FIRST WE EAT

Food, life, and more

Stories by Michele Sabad,
author of
Camp Follower: One Army Brat's Story

HTTPS://STEVIESZABAD.COM/

First We Eat 2020 by Michele Sabad. All rights reserved.

No part of this book may be used or reproduced in any manner whatsoever without written permission except in the case of brief quotations in critical articles and reviews. For more information, contact MESabad.
First edition.

Cover art, design, and interior sketches by Nathan Fréchette.
Typesetting and interior design by Éric Desmarais.
Edited by Cait Gordon.

Legal deposit, Library and Archives Canada, March 2020.

Paperback ISBN: 978-1-7751423-2-4
Ebook ISBN: 978-1-7751423-3-1

MESabad
https://stevieszabad.com/

Praise for "Camp Follower One Army Brat's Story"

"Michele really knows how to tell a story. A life that starts as a military brat and meanders into marriage, school and through [to] motherhood. From cover to cover I was engaged as she took me through familiar towns and incidents, to places I have never been and activities I have never experienced."

"If you want to know about growing up as a military 'brat' this is the story. It captures the life and the emotions perfectly. Thank you Michele for your gift."

"The life of a base "BRAT" is little known but also captures so much of the everyday life of regular people put in a rather odd situation. A good rendition of childhood and beyond in a world most people never know but which is so central to our lives and security. Touching, revealing, often comic sense of life in a series of upheavals and loyalties."

"For me, a U.S. Army brat, I found it interesting to get the perspective of a Canadian brat."

"A real page-turner... Highly recommend to all, even civvies who would like a glimpse into the Brat life."

"I could totally relate to this story, even though I'm from a different country. Just goes to show you we have more in common than not."

"Michele's writing style is easy to read yet not too simplistic. The illustrations for each chapter were perfect. This would be an ideal gift for a teen or older, especially one living the life attached to the military."

"Ordered it...received it...read it...loved it."

"Most of the reviews here are from "military brats" like the author, but even though I have never been in the military and after being thoroughly entertained by the read, I can say that anyone would enjoy this book...While the title will attract fellow military brats, I recommend 'Camp Follower: One Army Brat's Story' to anyone who just wants a good read."

"Great book! Michele writes with ease and humour, making her stories come alive. It's an easy read, following a real family, in settings most of us will never know. It opened up my eyes to military life and really how different it can be for the families who are 'rootless'. Highly recommend it! Read it, then Thank a soldier...and his family members."

"As a former army brat and a 12-year ground pounder... [Michele] hit it out of the park!!!!!"

This book is dedicated to Don.

Contents

Introduction	8
Coffee	12
House Coffee Recipe	17
Breakfast	19
Gourmet Oatmeal Recipe	25
Dairy Disasters	27
Chocolate Story	33
Chow Time	42
Implementing	46
Recipe Chapter – Sort Of	50
Hamburger Soup	51
Family Mush	54
Snack Nachos	58
Salads	59
Grilled Cheese	67
Spices	74
Caesar cocktail	79
My Rules	80
Best Meals of my Life	85
First Anniversary	87
The Steak Stories	90
The Best Appetizer	94
Restaurants	99
1960s	99
1970s	103
1980s: Girls Just Want to Have Fun	105
1990s	108
2000s	110

2010s	110
Beyond	111
Diet Chapter and Lessons from Women	113
The Doctor	118
The Diet Queens	120
The Party Girl Diet	121
The Women of Steel Diets	122
My Favourite Evil Food	125
Lessons from Kids and Dogs	129
D'Arcy and the Cookies and Pie	129
Sasha – The Rubber Child	135
Cognac	139
One Day in the (Food) Life.	144
Retirement Monday	145
Casino Wednesday	147
Giving Thanks and other Celebrations	149
Office Food	155
Christmas at the Office	159
Desserts	164
Drink, Drink	167
Alcohol	172
Generations and Change	177
Retirement	183
Grandma	186
Author's Afterword and Acknowledgements	190
About the Author	193

Introduction

Food. First, we eat. Then we live. We all must eat; life demands it. As a successful species, humans have become adept at providing food to fuel themselves wherever and whatever the circumstances. We've evolved to be clever and enterprising, and food is the never-ending quest, a continual obsession. We talk about food, fantasize about food, read about food. We desire it. We need it. We want it. We take pictures of food. Some of us have more food, more than we even need. Some not so much. This book will relay stories of one of us, this author, and stories of her life with food.

Stories. A requirement in a fulfilling life. Books, movies, plays for sure, but even daily gossip, social media posts, chats with strangers—all to convey the stories, big and small, of our lives. Arguably, life without stories, unlike life without food, is possible but not very fun. We live our stories. We blurb, we chat with cashiers about a souvenir grocery bag, we talk to the bus driver about the traffic delay, we discuss with strangers—the weather is a topic everyone can opine on. Our children's lives. Our health issues. Our recipes. All these are stories humans tell and absorb, because we are alive. We care and share a need to know, to learn, to figure out the world and our place in it. We may exaggerate, invent, even lie in our stories, to exchange ideas and information. We crave to know, to understand, to judge, to learn about life!

As a lucky Canadian, I've discovered the food history and stories of my family, my grandparents, and my European immigrant ancestors. Canada, the tossed salad of the world, has many food cultures to enjoy. But history and culture evolve, food preparation evolves, and so do the stories of them and with them. My father was in the Army, and then my husband was in the Air Force—there were unique family circumstances in this kind of life to contribute to my inventory of food stories. I grew up and lived all over the country and even out of it, from being born in Calgary, Alberta, to living in Germany and then back to Canada, to Labrador and Saskatchewan, Ontario, Manitoba, back to Alberta, and finally settled in my kids' hometown of Aylmer, a part of Gatineau, Québec in the National Capital region of Ottawa, Ontario. Cultural differences of a locale are always reflected in their food, so I've had quite the variety in my life: prairie family picnics, German *fasching* food (carnival food like chocolate cream puffs with wafer bottoms); Newfoundland fish feeds (Seal flipper pie. Did I really eat that or dream it?); Québec *cabanes à sucre* (maple sugar shacks) where suckers are made by rolling the thickened boiled syrup on a stick in the snow. Over a lifetime of six decades, I've also discovered my own ways with food. Providing and preparing sustenance is a daily act of life, and as society and technology changes, so do our food rituals. What we eat as children is almost certainly not what nor how we eat as adults. I've noticed that as I age, however, that I'm drifting back to those earlier times of my life with food. Ah, but what a journey, life—life and food!

One of my first memories is of eating a peanut butter sandwich with a cousin on the cement steps of someone's (Mine? His?) house. Summertime. Wearing shorts, my brown hair in pigtails. Swatting away flies (so probably at my cousin's home—all my cousins lived in the prairie countryside, rife with flies at every meal, especially, but not restricted to, outdoors). Do you recall, or did you know, that old homes with wooden window frames had small circular holes in the sill—or maybe the frame itself, I don't know—on the outside of the bottom of the window? Ventilation? I think they were winter storm windows, but not everyone changed them with the coming of summer; they were often painted shut. Anyway, sitting on that step, my cousin was eating his sandwich of soft white bread, and peeling off the crusts. And then he was taking those crusts and stuffing them into those little window frame holes under the window.

"What are you doing that for?" I must have asked, because I remember his answer, "I don't eat crusts!"

"Why not?"

"Because they put hair on your chest."

Oh! I looked down at my own sandwich in a new light.

And so go the stories of food and life. The life I've enjoyed and still enjoy is threaded with stories of food, as I'm sure is yours.

The accounts in this book are true and about me, as told by me, the author, but this is not simply a memoir. There are recipes of dishes or meals that I myself have created, but this is not a recipe book, nor a cookbook. There are stories of eating and types of food, and how I learned to manage my weight in our Western world of plenty, but this is most definitely not a diet book. There are tales with advice and lessons learned, but I wouldn't call it a self-help book. It's just a book of stories about food. A book I hope you will enjoy as I share them with you.

Coffee

L et's start the stories like I start the day—with coffee!

I'm retired from my career in Information Technology. It was good-paying work, but I don't miss it. Today, in my sixties, the new self-directed life of an author and storyteller to live, I begin every morning at home by making a pot of coffee. No-name, big-savings cannisters of fine ground coffee to make in the drip machine. Not 100% cheap store brand, though; I'll mix in a bag of Starbuck's or Van

Houtte or another such name brand, usually of a medium or stronger flavour to amp up the taste. As usual (you will see), I couldn't say what proportions of which kind I add on any particular day; I just know on some days my husband will say, "Wow, good coffee today!" And some days he won't. Rarely, but occasionally, he will say, "What's wrong with the coffee today?" Some days I will know why (I know when I overuse the scoop or underuse it), and some days I shrug because I won't have a clue. Or, I'll say, "If you don't like it, get up first and make it yourself." This is how marriages of over forty years work out well, because of course he'll apologize for criticizing the coffee if I suggest he should make it. It always smells wonderful, regardless, wafting down the hall to the bedroom and is sure to lure him out of bed in the morning. Yes, in marriages of over forty years, you lure each other *out* of bed.

    I wasn't allowed to drink coffee growing up; it was an "adult" drink. I could have tea after supper, with lots of milk. My mother, like her mother before her, served tea on the dinner table in a pot with a cozy on top. Cozy: a hand knit kind of teapot "sweater" to keep the tea hot. Our teacups came on saucers. My father, like his father before him, would pour his tea out of his cup and into his saucer to slurp it up. To cool it off, he would say, so I wondered, why the tea cozy on the pot to keep it so hot then? I still drink tea today, but with a dessert square of some type—a brownie or piece of pecan sugar pie—in the afternoon more likely now, and in a mug.

When I finally tried coffee as a grown-up, I found the taste icky—bitter, no matter how much sugar I added—and I hated the furry-mouth aftertaste (probably from too much sugar, I realize now). In college, most of my classmates drank coffee, and one girl I knew seemed to live on it; I never saw her eat any food. I also never saw her without a paper coffee cup in her hand, even in class. Even in the computer lab, where I was sure there was a sign that read, "No Food or Drink." I do remember the day she mentioned that she couldn't feel her face, or for that matter, the whole left side of her body. We sent her to Emergency, thinking, well, you know, the worst! But when she returned to class the next day, she said the doctor just told her to cut down on the caffeine.

It was only much later, in my late thirties, those middle adult years, raising boys, busy, that I discovered the medicinal benefits of the magical coffee bean.

I was working as an IT consultant, after countless years of university, college and moving around with my military husband's postings. Finally, I made good money at a large government department on the Québec side of the National Capital Region of Ottawa. Hectic weekends with two boys playing competitive hockey, made Mondays appreciated down-time days for me. The serenity of my little cubicle, tucked in the bowels of the government building where consultants were shoved, with Monday emails to read, weekend automated output to review, and the weekly schedule to plan, even though all the planning would most likely be bumped anyway by "Emergency Tuesday." Monday was never the busiest time at the office; busy would come later in the day and week as the programmers ran into their issues that I, as their Oracle Database Administrator, would have to address by abandoning said previously planned schedule. But despite my unusual affection for Mondays, they often heralded a sniffly nose due to overstressed hockey-parent weekends running around rinks, driving to out-of-town games, and squeezing in the house and grocery-shopping duties. The Monday sniffles could be followed on Tuesday with a sore throat, and by Thursday I might be so stuffed up in the sinuses that in desperation to feel better for the rapidly-approaching weekend with all its recurring commitments, I'd run downstairs to the doctor in the mall pharmacy to see if there was anything to be done. Of course, there wasn't—it was always a viral sinus infection: tough it out, get rest, drink fluids, get rest. Hah, rest! Then at one of these useless medical visits, the nurse casually asked if I had any allergies, or was there perhaps any asthma in the family?

Yes, we're a family of asthma, and allergies, and eczema and psoriasis. I myself didn't suffer too much with them, maybe springtime allergies, some major childhood eczema, but all was under control now, as long as I didn't overdo the wonderful Body

Shop soaps and butters with all their delicious fragrances.

"Why?" I asked.

"Oh, a family history of asthma can be related to recurrent sinus infections, is all," she informed me.

Really? I soon did my own research and discovered that coffee had once been used as a traditional medicine for asthmatics in the past, before better drugs were available. Coffee as medicine? I was intrigued. It couldn't hurt, so the next afternoon around 2:30 pm, I went to get my "work husband" Dave, from his corner cubicle where he nested, hunched, barricaded behind boxes of hardware and wires. Dave was the Systems Administrator, another lonely technical position, but one that I, as the DBA, needed to work with to get things done for the programmers. Dave was fiercely protective of his computers and their realms and considered them his personal domain. I used to joke that our jobs would be easier without programmers and business clients using the systems, but to Dave it wasn't a joke—he meant it. Dave drank coffee, usually alone at his desk, but as I said, I needed him on my good side and often dragged him out of his cubby once a day for human interaction and coffee. On this break, I took a deep breath, and ordered one too.

Icky. But cream and sugar helped. Not too much sugar. It was bitter, but on probation as medicine, so I stuck it out. Gross. But.

But something happened. That afternoon, I

was able to comprehend and sort out solutions to the late-day database issues that the computer programmers liked to save up for the last hour of work; no need to pile them up for the next morning's investigations. Then I'm off work at 4:00 p.m. to drive to the gym before getting home by 6:00 p.m., when my wonderful real husband would have already picked up boys from school and started supper. And instead of dreading the elliptical machine at the club, I surprise myself by doing the full twenty minutes instead of cheating down to fifteen. A refreshing shower later, then staying awake until the 9:00 p.m. TV show finished—was all this new late-day life the result of my 2:30 p.m. coffee break, which now included coffee?

I was a convert. I never did suffer another sinus infection. Today I'm a happy addict.

House Coffee Recipe

The most important ingredient in this recipe: use your favourite coffee mug. Right now (I will change my mind from time to time), mine is a smallish, sturdy white restaurant-style hearty, happy mug. It originated in the morning room from a Québec hotel chain where we stayed many times as hockey parents in years gone by. I don't remember "borrowing" it from the hotel. In fact, I think my father took it back to his hotel room on a visit and forgot it at our house later. I think this because whenever he visits, he uses this cup with the exclamation, "Oh, I remember that cup! D'Arcy's hockey tournament...in Sherbrooke, wasn't it?" Maybe because I'm a new grandmother now myself, I'm nostalgic for those younger parenting times, and so am choosing this cup lately. If so, that would be a good thing about growing older: remembering the good parts of the past, not all the crazy bad parts, like some that those hockey parents had!

Now make your home coffee. Mine is brewed drip coffee. I scoop as much or as little grounds as I feel like that day. After the bubbling and brewing (during which you're cleaning up the counters from last night's television time snacks), pour into that favourite mug. Add splashes of non-dairy creamer, vanilla-flavoured. Add one square of dark chocolate per cup, stir until melted. (If it doesn't melt well, buy more expensive dark chocolate.) Top up with 2% lactose-free milk until you like the colour. I like it fairly milky. You'll see why the lactose-free later.

Have another cup!

Breakfast

Growing up the eldest and only girl with three brothers, I can't remember a time I didn't make my own breakfast. We were a typical military family of the 1960s and '70s; we lived in rented housing on military bases called PMQs. That stood for Married Quarters—it still is debated whether the P was for Personal or Private or Permanent, but whatever it meant, we called our houses PMQs anyway. I doubt they meant Permanent, because we moved every two to three years. Maybe permanent applied to the house structure itself. It certainly had a permanent (as in exactly the same) post-WW2-style on every military base I ever lived on.

It's not fair to say I always made my own breakfast, because stay-at-home Mom did get up and make Dad's breakfast in my youth, so she must have made mine also. It's just that with baby brothers coming every couple of years, requiring their baby-food attention, and with Dad needing a big breakfast of eggs and coffee before heading off to his sergeant job at the gym (he was a PTI, a Physical Training Instructor), I know I'd been absolutely capable of feeding myself before heading off to school, usually paired with my one-year-younger brother, Mark. He was (Still is?) a peanut-butter fanatic, and could eat toast and peanut-butter for every meal, especially with jam. Not me. I will eat peanut-butter today, but back then, only occasionally. Same for the jam (just sometimes and then spread thinly). I didn't like seeds getting stuck in my teeth all day. We all ate toast though, even if just with margarine for me. If I had to name one food only that everyone in our family ate at any time of the day, it would be toast. I once offered a college friend some toast as a snack when she visited. She still laughs about that, "Who serves guests a piece of toast?" I didn't and still don't know what she found amusing.

Along with toast, there was always cold cereal with milk. Especially on weekends, when Mom and Dad would sleep in. Mom always bought special "weekend" cereal for us to go with the cartoons on TV, and there were no restrictions on amounts allowed on Saturday mornings. (Well, we had TV before we moved to Germany. There, no TV so comic books instead.) I loved Captain Crunch. My teeth hurt today remembering the pasty sugar stuck in every crevice. It needed lots of milk and time to go soggy the way I preferred. I never understood the commercials that advertised the crunch; I liked the sog. My brothers ate any sugary cereal—Sugar Crisp, Alpha-Bits—and added spoonsful more. Their bowl would be so loaded with the white crystals, they could scrape sludge off the bottom, having achieved over-saturation levels for the liquid. Any wonder my generation has heavily restored dental work and high rates of Type 2 diabetes?

But that was weekends. Weekday cereal would be healthier, like Corn Flakes, Rice Crispies, or Puffed Wheat. Oh, and Muffets—muffin-sized spun wheat crisps that were a precursor to today's Mini-Wheats. I liked them soaked first in hot water then drained. That sog-factor again. And still spoonful of sugar added!

The most memorable breakfasts of my youth included porridge. We lived in some darn cold places: Calgary, Alberta; Goose Bay, Labrador; and Yorkton, Saskatchewan, to name some of my pre-teen home locales. So, winters in Canada required those porridge mornings.

Yes, we always called the hot pot of grey matter bubbling on the stove porridge, not oatmeal. I liked porridge. Sometimes my mother would make a pot of Red River cereal, very gritty with flax seeds in it, and I loved that even more. With brown sugar and milk, a big bowlful came with mom's advice to "Eat up, it'll stick to your ribs," which, like admonitions such as "It'll put hair on your chest," are not always clever things to say to a child. I didn't want anything stuck to my ribs, thank you. Of course, porridge would always be accompanied by toast and margarine; we'd dip the toast in the porridge. Later, in our teens, Mom would buy the packets you could make yourself—she was a working mom by then—so we'd pick our own packet flavour, maybe even Cream of Wheat, which was good with syrup on it. I stopped eating the Cream of Wheat, though, when I entered my knowledgeable teenage years, becoming so much smarter than everyone else about everything, including nutrition. Cream of Wheat didn't have enough fibre, of which, I informed everyone, we needed to eat more. I'm sure you've all known such teenage creatures: the ones who know everything. Funny that many years later while travelling on vacation in the southern United States, I was eager to try grits, having never had them. Turns out, they're just like Cream of Wheat.

There were many years after leaving home when I did not eat oatmeal. I married, went to university and college, then finally Don, my husband, and I became wealthier with better jobs, so we ate too much bacon and eggs or muffins and bagels for a few years. Oatmeal? Bah, that's *poor people* food. We were on our way to our western lifestyle middle-aged spreads and nascent health concerns. But becoming a mother myself dragged me back to those family-style breakfasts with their better nutrition, and I would cook up a pot of Quaker oats for my young daycare children, wearing a housecoat over my work attire in the mornings to do so. As the cycle of life progressed, my own children made their own oatmeal packets in the mornings, and it even became a snack food after school or after hockey games. Apples and cinnamon were favourites, as was the maple sugar flavoured one.

I can't help but mention that my boys were, like

my brothers before them, voracious eaters. Are all boys? In my experience, yes.

My son, D'Arcy wasn't quite two years old when he started at daycare. We'd all get up and have a bowl of oatmeal at the table together—his bowlful was just as big as mine—with toast and juice. Don and I didn't drink coffee at home yet. We drank grapefruit juice, made from frozen concentrate. Old South was the name brand, better than the no-name kind.

The Kinder Care Mini School daycare had been a wonderful place, colourful and bright on those cold, dark, workday mornings in Winnipeg. Despite a few pretend sulks when he first started there, D'Arcy soon rushed in with enthusiasm in the mornings. We dropped him off before 8:00 a.m., then Don would drop me off at work downtown before heading back to the air base for his own day in the military. An early routine, but we'd all started with a filling breakfast at home. So, it was a surprise to me when the daycare teacher pulled me aside on one of those early days to say,

"Can you please send breakfast in with your son in the morning? He's so hungry when he shows up."

"What do you mean? D'Arcy eats a full breakfast just before he comes. Oatmeal and toast and juice. And you feed them a morning snack here anyway, at 9:30 a.m.!"

"Oh, really? He's already eaten? But he's stealing from the other kids who bring their breakfast when he gets here. And he gobbles up the snack later, too."

I was perplexed at first, then embarrassed. I looked into my son's shiny green eyes grinning at me, and realized yes, he could eat and then eat some more. I adjusted the morning suitcase. (Our car looked packed for a trip every day, with husband's and my gym bags, plus daycare bag of diapers and toddler paraphernalia, now to be added into a snack bag of Cheerios, and cheese strings, a juice box, and whatever else. Another piece of toast? For the road!) The daycare used to give a short daily report filled in with food amounts eaten, like, "Finished 1 helping," or "Had seconds." D'Arcy's results soon said "2+" under that heading, meaning more than two helpings!

Retired from the scheduled working world, I've gone back to eating oatmeal a few times a week. Health reasons nowadays. Oatmeal is fibre-full, and I'm told it helps keep cholesterol levels in check. I'm reminded of the Tragically Hip song about blowing high dough and stretching it out the less you have left. Like running out of money, when you're running out of years, you want to make them last. So now my oatmeal, like my life, has been upgraded to make the smaller years left last. I even call it "gourmet" oatmeal, not porridge anymore. Here's my recipe; I don't apologize for the detail and time it takes to make, as that's another pleasure of retirement—taking the time.

Gourmet Oatmeal Recipe

Note about quantities: I use what looks about right. Do what you think is best.

Ingredients

- Old-fashioned rolled oats
- Apple, cut into bite-sized chunks. I use McIntosh for best, tart flavour. Paula Reds also work well, and they keep their crunch.
- Dried cranberries (the secret sweetener ingredient)
- Cinnamon, nutmeg, allspice
- Chopped walnuts
- 2% lactose-free milk

Method (oatmeal for two people: one "normal eater" and one husband-sized)

1. Run cold water in a small pot. How much? I turn the tap on full and count to four.
2. Put the pot on the stovetop burner, on high heat.
3. Scoop the oats into the pot and stir.
4. Based on how you feel, add more oats. Four tablespoons aren't usually enough, so I wing it after that. But don't overdo it because the oats really, really swell up. In fact, the first few times you try this "recipe" (I use the term loosely for obvious reasons), maybe follow the instructions for quantities as prescribed by Mr. Quaker on the package.
5. Keep stirring up the pot.

6. Put the apple chunks in a bowl, then add the dried cranberries.
7. The pot should be boiling by now, turn it down, but keep up the low boil.
8. Time to throw the apples and cranberries in. Keep stirring.
9. Get the walnuts and cinnamon and nutmeg out.
10. Check the oatmeal while stirring. If it's too thick, add a splash more water. It's too late to add more oats if it's too thin. (When I mistakenly make it too thin, I just pretend it's gruel, a word I always think means "oatmeal soup.")
11. Done after about five minutes of boiling. Scoop into the two bowls.
12. Toss as many walnuts as you can afford on top. This expensive and healthful ingredient is what makes the oatmeal "gourmet".
13. Sprinkle heavily with cinnamon and nutmeg. Add allspice if you have it.
14. Add 2% lactose-free milk. Or even whole milk. Don't use skim, enjoy the yummy richness of the milk fat.

It's not your grandma's porridge!

Dairy Disasters

It's time to explain why I will specify lactose-free milk in my recipes and stories.

I've always loved dairy, the creamier the better. I grew up in the days of no percentages listed on milk cartons; milk was just milk, all whole of it. And ice cream? Truly ambrosia, a gift from the gods. Ice cream, when bought in those old cardboard blocks and sitting in the frosty freezer of my childhood homes, would never last longer than a day or two after the payday purchase. Luckily, my parents loved ice cream, too, so there were always some coins to scrounge when the tinkle of the ice cream truck in Calgary sent us running for our nickels, then out into the street amid screams of anticipatory ecstasy. Fudgesicle for my brother and creamsicle, the orange popsicle coating over vanilla ice cream, for me. A drumstick for my mother, sometimes. She wasn't as crazy for ice cream as the rest of us. A revel (the vanilla bar coated in chocolate crust) for my dad, who ran with us to the truck as fast as any of the other neighbourhood kids. When we moved to Germany, the ice cream truck did actual scoops of real ice cream, though, into tiny little wafer cones. Just as good.

Returning to Canada for a posting to Goose Bay, I remember a wonderful stewardess on the long airplane ride bringing me all the glasses of milk I wanted. Ten-year-old me dreamed of being a stewardess back then.

Yogurt was my cool snack of choice as a teenager, when I'd begun thinking of eating healthier (in between potato chips and chocolate bars, of course.) I even got a yogurt-making appliance for a birthday present one year in Petawawa.

Once older and married, skim milk became available—all of us diet-conscious young women switched to it. One got used to the watery taste. Fat, including milk fat, was out. Skinny was in.

Except for ice cream, of course. Dairy Queen never gave up her crown as a royal treat destination. Hot fudge brownie sundaes shared with my boyfriend who had a car and could drive into Pembroke for the delight. Calories? I can only imagine: a long, giant pull of that rich soft vanilla ice cream, drowned in hot fudge sauce ladled on top, then festooned on the sides with not one, but two full-sized squares of walnut-encrusted brownies. Did I really eat a whole sundae like that myself? What is the teenage metabolism, anyway, some kind of freak of nature? It should be bottled and sold as magic.

Cheese hardly seems worth mentioning as dairy. To me, it was its own food group. It belonged on sandwiches for school lunches as processed slices, and Velveeta for paydays. Pizza: the cheesier, the better. Real blocks of cheese: old, white, and orange cheddar cubes cut up on plates, stabbed with toothpicks for picnics and holidays. I remember buying chunks of good cheeses, wrapped in red wax, as Christmas presents. I don't remember when I discovered Swiss cheese, or any kind with holes, but it was my favourite. It smelled funky on my fingers, in a good way, after cutting it into snack-sized chunks.

Looking back, I think I first noticed my dairy digestion issues in college. I would scoop cottage cheese with canned peaches from the salad bar for lunch almost daily. But sometimes in the afternoon, I'd be very uncomfortable, with repressed gas rolling around in my stomach, often as loud as if I'd un-repressed it, especially in a quieter after-lunch class.

"Hey, who farted?" a thoughtful classmate once

whispered, but of course loud enough for others to turn and look.

Embarrassed, I must have blushed purple and never sat near this young fellow again. I suffered many an afternoon with an upset stomach, holding gas in until I could get out of class and walk to the parking lot to my car, letting loose and relieving all the bloating pressure. I loved that little Datsun 200SX, with the cassette tape player with auto-reverse. It was my refuge, and my release, in every way. I would be fine after the drive home and forget my afternoon ordeal. It only happened after lunch at school, and since I was still drinking skim milk at home, I didn't connect any of the dairy dots to my problem.

Fast-forward to working life in my early thirties. Yes, I sometimes noticed the painful effects after nachos, or creamy restaurant meals. I was so sick after one such evening out with friends that my husband had to take me home and we considered a stop at the hospital along the way. I thought I was having a gall bladder attack or some other such serious event. But no, after a gassy release—unpleasant for my poor husband—I'd be fine. And so it went. Clueless, thinking fatty foods were the issue, I continued the random suffering, eating and drinking dairy as usual. The skim milk still wasn't yet affecting me. Soon after quitting my reliable but boring government job to become a consultant, however, I started having the now familiar gurgly stomach shortly after arriving at work in the morning, and it would be a bother until after lunch (and after a lunch-time with no dairy and a walk outside, where all could be released.) *I must be suffering from the stress of the new high-pressure workload*, I reasoned. The fresh air walk for a pleasant afternoon proved that, didn't it? I was fine on weekend mornings. Also proof that my job was the cause of my digestive disorders, right?

On weekend mornings, I would usually forgo a breakfast of cereal and skim milk. Just toast with peanut butter and juice, more leisurely while I read magazines and the kids watched TV. (I wasn't yet a coffee drinker at home). Or we'd all have a big weekend feed of scrambled eggs and bacon. It seems obvious and ridiculous to me today, that I didn't realize it could be dairy products that were causing me these years of grief.

My mother didn't drink milk. I remember nagging her that she needed the calcium, but her response was simply, "I don't like milk. I get enough in my coffee." Of course, smarter than I was, she probably knew milk didn't agree with her. Stubborn to a fault, it took me longer to figure it out and to realize it wasn't uncommon to be lactose intolerant. Also, it could be inherited, and the symptoms could vary or become worse over time. Some kinds of dairy were fine for some people for a certain period of time. Like me lasting with skim milk for longer than with cottage cheese.

Unlike in my mother's day, I found lactase enzyme pills at the drugstore, and surprise, surprise, taking them with my cereal on workdays worked. No more stomach aches until lunchtime. And over time, I found lactose-free milk. Today, even many cheeses come in lactose-free varieties. So, when my son in his early thirties announced that no thanks, no pizza for him, he was lactose intolerant, I was amazed that he had figured it out himself so quickly. Sometimes I have great hope for humanity when I see such progression in our young people.

Now if only Dairy Queen would offer their soft-serve in a lactose-free version! I hope I live long enough for that.

Chocolate Story

S peaking of delicious:
"Mom, wake up, can I have my allowance? Please? And Mark's."

It was a normal Saturday morning, after breakfast and cartoons. Parents sleeping in. Baby brothers still in their cribs. Time to get on with the best part of the week. Allowance day! Candy run!

In the early 1960s, children as young as six and seven years old (Mark's and my ages) could walk the bigger streets to the Safeway grocery store near our military homes, our PMQs in Sarcee, Calgary, Alberta. I say bigger streets. That only meant no sidewalk, and lots of traffic, especially on a Saturday. Perhaps in recollection, the road wasn't the super-highway of memory because really, did our parents let us walk a super-highway alone? I don't think we had to cross the bigger street anyway, so it must have been fine.

After mom sleepily gropes around the nightstand to take her change purse out of the drawer, she would hand me a couple of dimes or maybe a quarter, to be shared with my obedient little brother. At least he'd been obedient at allowance time! Then off we trotted, out of the dim row house where parents were clunking awake to feed screaming littler brothers, down the cement steps into the brightness of the courtyard, over to the side street, to follow it straight down to the bigger street. Off on our Saturday quest for candy at Safeway.

Ten cents could buy quite the treats in 1965. I was pretty consistent: either a chocolate bar (five cents) plus gum, or a new box of crayons, despite the hefty ten cent price. My little brothers were always breaking or eating my crayons, and I loved those waxy wands when new and straight and store-sharp with the paper still intact enough to sound out the creative colour descriptions. Goldenrod. Periwinkle. Sienna. Burnt and Raw Sienna. (What was a Sienna?) Anyway, I couldn't resist chocolate enough to buy crayons every week, so having selected my favourite bar, a Crispy Crunch or Milky Way, I'd wait for Mark to decide what he wanted, which was usually something sugary-crystally-coated. Sometimes we'd buy a plastic toy from the machine where you'd put your nickel in the slot, then crank the handle around to release a toy soldier or farm animal. Like the crayons, our collections of plastic soldiers and animals was always declining due to loss in the sandboxes. But also like the crayons, we couldn't afford these too often either because we needed our candy fix. Dilemmas, dilemmas!

I've read there are two kinds of people: those who can delay gratification, and those who won't. I am definitely one who can delay. Even at seven years old, I would wait until a good, alone time at home to open my chocolate bar. I'd try to make Mark wait to eat any of his candy, but I'm sure he wolfed it all down within minutes of home arrival. Myself? One, maybe two bites for the day. Then careful rewrapping to hide the rest of the bar somewhere in my room, my own room as the oldest and only girl, the remainder of the treasure to be enjoyed in careful portions over the next days. My brothers were clever scavengers, however, and I became adept at the hiding places. Nothing infuriated me more than realizing my stash had been looted. These habits of delaying the best treats, and hiding treats for future enjoyment, plus the anger of anyone interrupting such planning, would play out in my adult professional life far into the unimagined future, as we will see later in this story.

For now, candy was an important addition to my life. And chocolate ranked at the top of my candy pyramid.

We grow up. I moved away from my candy-stealing brothers, to a candy-stealing husband. (What can you do?). Candy wasn't what adults ate, so I graduated to snacks and treats, especially at work.

Have you ever worked in an open cubicle-style office? Or at least watched the TV show *The Office*? Snacks are an integral part of the day, especially sweets and especially by 3:00 p.m. In my hockey mom years when I was required to sell chocolate bars for fundraising, I would bring cases of the stuff to work to hide under my desk until 3:00 p.m., at which time coworkers would immediately sense, maybe even smell (with the instincts of a family dog), the boxes of chocolate stacked at the corner of my desk. I could sell out my quota before the end of the week.

Just like when I was a child, I could make a chocolate bar at work last all week. Ah, but with better chocolate. Only dark chocolate, and only the kind you could buy in specialty stores, not at the corner store. Kinds with percentages of cocoa listed on the label. Kinds where two squares a day was satisfying.

"Why do you only eat two squares of chocolate?" asked a coworker. I was a thirty-something computer programmer working in Cold Lake, Alberta, my first government job. Coffee break was practically a scheduled meeting. At 2:30ish every afternoon, all the civilian women in the office (only about four of us, and I was the only computer programmer; the others being the secretary to the colonel, and human resource clerks) would meet in the lunch room and make coffee or tea (for me, coffee was still in my future) and chat about the day, our kids, our diets.

"Yeah, where's the rest of that chocolate bar?" another asked.

"In my desk. I only eat a few bites with my tea. It's all I want." Really, it was.

I don't think they believed me.

I'm not sure why when I could afford it, I didn't go for quantity instead of quality, but I did. Better one three-dollar chocolate bar than three dollars' worth of cheap bars. Conditioned to better chocolate, I began to regard my old Crispy Crunches and their ilk as plastic by comparison, not worthy enough to waste calories on. I was happy and enjoyed my couple of bites but noticed not everyone understood my self-imposed snack rules. Their awe was uncomfortable, and it's always been hard enough to fit in. I was a military spouse after having been a military child, moving every couple of years in and out of schools and jobs and cliques. I was used to adapting to the ways of others as I aimed to belong. But I stuck to many of my own ways, too. They had served me well so far in this nomadic lifestyle.

We grow older. I became less concerned with the opinions of others, thank goodness. I even found like-spirited food-rule-makers and fellow chocoholics at one job. I wasn't the only strange person in the world with odd food habits, hallelujah!

I was an Oracle DBA, a specialized IT consultant, working in a big government department. These were high-powered working years, teaming with my officer husband to support two sons about to enter their most expensive years of sports, driving, and university. Stressful years, when I think back, but they are far enough back now that I can smile about it.

My desk was in an open-office-style room with about six or seven of us spread around, all consultants. I shared a tabletop with another consultant, a programmer named Michel, who we called Mike so as not to confuse him with myself, the girl Michele. Mike was a wine connoisseur who regaled us with stories of the dinner wines he and his France-French wife would have with their European-style suppers each evening after they put their children to bed.

"An excellent Bordeaux, it went perfectly with the pork chops we broiled." And like that.

On days he rode his bike to work, Mike would mark an X on the calendar on his side of the cubicle then add up the X's at the end of the month. Each marked a ten dollar or so savings in parking, and the monthly total would be his wine budget for the following month. I was impressed. It sounded like the kind of self-disciplined food-life rule that I myself could have invented. Mike was an odd guy, but in a good way.

Mike noticed I only ate good quality dark chocolate, a few bites at a time, with my coffee break in the afternoon, which we mostly had at our desks, being so busy all the time.

"What kind of chocolate is that, Michele?" Mike asked one day. I showed him the wrapper. There was a mall downstairs in the building complex where we worked with a food court and specialty shops that sold all kinds of chocolate and candy snacks for the public servants who worked above.

"It's only a 70%," he intoned, handing back the wrapper. "I prefer 85."

"I like 85, but not all the time. Sometimes I like the creamier texture of the 70-72."

"Eighty-five can be creamier. The lower ones are too sweet, usually. Depends on the brand. I've never tried this kind."

"Be my guest." I offered the bar. He broke out a square, careful to do so while keeping his hands on the tinfoil part of the wrapper, and tasted it.

"Not bad. A little too sweet for me. But a nice, nutty undertone." He looked at the wrapper again.

The next day, Mike joined a couple of us in the food court to pick up our coffees. He bought a different kind of chocolate bar "to taste-test and compare" with what I still had left upstairs. It was the beginning of our daily chocolate-rating event. The others in the office got into it. We'd all have a square of the daily two or three bars to compare, then discuss and rate them. Too bitter, too heavy, doesn't melt easily. Just sweet enough, nice blend, good texture. We'd use pushpins to tack the wrappers of the different brands on the wall behind, the best ones at the top, and down to poorer-rated ones below. Discussions could be heated, but all in good fun. It was a refreshing break before the heavy last hours of the workday. Visitors to the office, usually our business clients, questioned the wall décor, but enjoyed the occasional participation in the daily ritual.

Our boss was a government employee named Benny. He'd drop in around a few times a day, sometimes with work or instructions; more often just to hang out. He had a stressful job on his side of the office, too.

As in most open offices, we kept bowls of candy in neutral areas, and Benny loved candy. I'd seen him put away handfuls from a box of Turtles one Christmas season. Fascinated, we kept handing him the box as we chatted, curious to see how many he'd eat. In fact, as I think about it, our office candy bowl was a big reason for his daily drop-ins. He always went right for the bowl, and shook it around if it was empty, looking annoyed, chirping us about it while ordering someone to go to the monthly business client meeting to take minutes for him. Lately, we'd been storing our expensive dark chocolate bars in the bowl in preparation for the late-day coffee break and taste-testing. But if Benny came in, he'd open wrappers and gobble up half a bar at a time without breaking a sweat. The longer he hung around, the more he'd eat.

Now, Benny was a good guy…and our boss. We couldn't tell him to stop eating our expensive coffee break treats. We had another solution.

Everyone knew by then that chocolate is not naturally sweet. Sugar is added. The higher the cocoa content, the less sugar and the more bitter and chalky. I can't remember whose idea it was because the whole group was in on it, but we bought a bar of 95% cocoa. And placed a large square of it, opened, right on top of the rest of our stash. As expected, when Benny next showed up, he unconsciously grabbed it right away and shoved it in his mouth.

He always chewed the chocolate, too, never letting the aromas and tastes melt in the mouth first, the way we all practiced. The reaction was immediate and priceless.

"Eww, what is this shit?" He tried to spit it out into his hand, but the texture was dry and pasty, and he ran over to a desk for a Kleenex to spit into. And then he looked for water, and ran from the room, obviously to get some.

Innocently, the next time Benny dropped by, we asked if he wanted more chocolate, but he didn't. We did continue to buy boxes of Turtles, though, just for him. None of the rest of us "chocolate snobs" now considered that stuff edible anymore.

Chow Time

Because food and culture are so intertwined, I've noticed in my travels that even among English speakers, there are different words used for the same things. Chips in England are French fries in Canada. Soda pop can be soft drinks, or soda or pop, depending on where you drink it. (It's pop to me, by the way.) Dressing, stuffing? What do you call the highly-personalized recipes of starchy, spiced fixings inside a cooked turkey? I could go on, but here are some words I use for another aspect of the food world: the mealtimes.

When we eat is as interesting as what we eat. Mealtimes have names, and many of the names are unique to locale. Siesta is the name for the time after midday meals in some cultures, for example. It gets its name from the Latin *sexta hora*, that is, the sixth hour of the day. Curious, I wonder when is considered the first hour of the day? There are certainly mealtimes that vary from my own traditions. We visited France recently. By 5:00 p.m., I was hungry and looking for restaurants for supper. The hotel receptionist was aghast—*Who eats that early?!* She informed me that restaurants don't even open for dinner until 7:00 p.m. Don't ask me where everyone in France hung out after work until then because the streets seemed deserted. Maybe they nap before dinner? I doubt my hard-working peasant ancestors could've waited until 7:00 p.m. to eat, unless that is the reason for teatime? Or was that an upper-class-only mealtime? My grandmother said a small sandwich and tea at 4:00 p.m. was simply "civilized." She wasn't from any upper-class background as far as I knew. And she didn't indulge in teatime often because she needed to cook a large farm meal for the working men for suppertime at 5:00 p.m. Unless it was harvest, or spring seeding, or a summer weeding; then supper wasn't until well after sundown. I remember she cooked a huge lunch when the men came in from the fields at midday and sent sandwiches back out with them, with thermoses of tea. I guess for their teatime?

I learned some meal names from my own parents and society, but all cultures evolve with priorities, so others I've created or use myself (like Second Breakfast—I stole that from *The Office*, who I'm told must have stolen that from the Hobbits in *Lord of the Rings*). Here is the list of mealtimes that may occur in my household. I say *may* because I try not to eat eight meals a day. Although I have.

Breakfast. Eaten as soon as you get up, to break the longest fast of the diurnal cycle–during sleep.

Second Breakfast. Am I the only person who

is hungriest about two hours after getting out of bed? No matter that I've already eaten breakfast two hours earlier? I like second breakfast better than breakfast. I'm hungrier at that time than at breakfast. It can be anything, from a sandwich to a pastry or any dessert-type item, with (more) coffee.

Lunch. Can be called dinner, as in "dinnertime." I'm mostly unimaginative with lunches—sandwiches, salads, soups—at home or on the go. The biggest change in lunches I've made is to order Vietnamese soup, or pho, for lunch. Especially after swimming; it's so satisfying, tasty, and exotic, yet familiar. I grew up eating soup for lunch at home. Although, if a bagged school or work lunch is required for the day's activities, it is likely a sandwich. I remember a college friend who shared a locker with me asking, "Is that processed cheese slice sandwich wrapped in the bread bag the same one you brought the first day of class?", as in "the exact same one", not just the same kind every day. It was just the same kind?

Afternoon snack. No explanation required here. Usually a sweet (chocolate always works) with tea or coffee.

Lupper. This is not a meal eaten every day, but it has its uses. It's a full-sized meal, like supper, usually eaten when real lunch is missed for some reason, or when a supper will not be available either at all or until very late (in the second supper time slot.) Served between 2:00–4:00 p.m. This was a popular meal during the years of raising hockey players; they needed lots of food, but it had to be scheduled around game times.

Teatime. If Lupper slipped to 4:00 p.m., I'd remember to call the mealtime "teatime" in honour of Grandma. But really, if the meal was a true lupper, it would just be early supper. And if it was smaller, it was just after-school snacks.

Supper. Also, like lunch, can be called dinner. We usually "go out for dinner." Again, this is very traditional for me: meat, starch, veggies, eaten around 5:00 p.m., when possible, although it can slip to as late as 6:00 p.m. Anything later means we probably had lupper earlier. So, there'd be no supper today, just second supper or snacks.

Second supper. No such thing, really, although we use the term, especially when it involves large plates and leftovers, as in leftovers from lupper. Eating after supper, however, is usually snacking, no matter what the food or what the quantities. It usually starts with holding cupboard doors open and saying, "Isn't there anything to eat around here?" This has been traditional junk food time: chips, sweets, alcohol, leftovers. It is also the mealtime I struggle with controlling; it serves no contribution to health, unless you count pure pleasure as contributing to health, and really, who doesn't? It definitely is the meal to miss if you're counting calories, but I swear, I have never been able to give it up for long.

Implementing

Sometimes, what we eat on, what we eat with, how things are served, what the serving dish looks like, and even temperature can influence the meal just as much as the food itself. For example: You're sitting with friends. You are serving a steaming wood-fired pizza on the Sunday-best platter, with cloth napkins. Ruby-red wine waits to be poured from a decanter into crystal glasses, glossy stainless-steel knives and forks gleam at the sides of the white matching set of plates; a side spinach salad sits in a central bowl with long-handled tongs at the ready. This sit-down meal could be considered a dinner. Eating the same pizza out of the cardboard delivery box while snuggled in a blanket to watch a Netflix movie, with a tumbler of wine poured from the 1.5 litre jug from the cupboard...well...is this dinner? I guess so, but you get my point.

    I'm sentimental about my food-delivery and presentation instruments. I have favourite plates for dinner, dessert, and for company. I have favourite glasses, too: one for water, one for milk, wine glasses, and cocktail glasses. I have favourite coffee cups. Favourite bowls. I have my mother's large serving platter that only comes out on Christmas and Thanksgiving or for family company. Why are these things so important? Perhaps because food itself is such a vital part of life, so repetitively necessary, yet each individual meal such a fleeting experience, the serving instruments themselves take on their own significance, as in *"les aides memoire"* of our lives, which include food every day.

    Cutlery, for example. I'm old enough to remember the real hardware that used to be provided on airlines for inflight meals of chicken or fish. Now, if any cutlery is required at all for the pita wrapped sandwich and vacuum-packed cheese chunks, it will be plastic. If they serve any food at all.

    I recently opened the "knives and forks drawer" at my son's house after pulling out all the wrong drawers first and yelling, "Where's your knives and forks drawer?" Just as my daughter-in-law yelled back, "The one beside the sink," I pulled open their version of my own such drawer. A plastic tray dividing knives, forks, spoons. An open side part with larger knives and serving spoons and miscellaneous openers, straws, and other unknown instruments. As I dug around the smaller spoons looking for one to stir my coffee with, I noticed a single soup-sized spoon with a rosette pattern down the handle. I picked it up. Smooth and silky, the pattern that used to have a darker background, now worn shinier than I remembered, the heavier weight reminding me of the quality, this spoon had been part of a magnificent set of cutlery for eight that my father had won at a curling bonspiel in Goose Bay, Labrador, in 1969. My mother had been so pleased. It came in a suitcase-style box lined with faux velvet, each glittering piece of metal its own work of art. It resided in a special drawer in the dining room, in the buffet. It was understood that these knives and forks (and spoons) were to be used only for special occasions. Of course, over the years, over the many military moves, most of that set migrated to living in the regular knives and forks drawers, and the migrating wouldn't end at my parents' place. I myself still had a few pieces, forty-some years after leaving home. Today, I don't remember giving this spoon to D'Arcy and Jess, but of course when young people set out to live on their own, like I did, they hoist a few necessities, like knives and forks, from their home planet, that is, from Mom's and Dad's knives and forks drawers. Happy at the sudden memories, blinking a tear away, I smiled and put the spoon back in the mix. Then I chose a teaspoon and closed the drawer.

Like me, you must have special food implements. Spoons, maybe, but I also have a copper-bottomed stovetop stainless steel pot that was given to me by my mother-in-law from her own collection in the first year of my marriage, because we just couldn't afford one to cook our soup in. It came with a lid, which years ago lost its Bakelite handle, and as a result was unusable, although we tried for a few years to lift it with oven mitts. I have since bought a newer set of cooking pots, expensive, with glass lids and stainless-steel lid handles, but my old pot with the black handle is still sturdy and the best for stirring up the gourmet oatmeal. I don't need the lid for that. Or for putting on a can of soup.

Recipe Chapter - Sort Of

I suppose we've all seen them, the "easy, fast, economical" recipes. In magazines, on the internet, from friends and family.

Well, I've never followed recipes, and I am suspicious about the hype. If it's so fast and cheap, how can it be good? Over the years when I compliment someone about a dish they serve, a common reaction is, "Oh, it's so easy to make! I'll give you the recipe." I've learned to stop saying, "Don't bother, I won't make it," because people tend to be offended by this honest answer. So, now I just say, "Haha, you know me; I can't cook! No thanks, don't bother."

Sometimes they will insist, and I am forced to accept, only to toss the information later. It's not being rude, it's just that I don't really need recipes to come up with healthy dishes I like. I don't care if food tastes exactly the same every time, so ingredients and quantities are not important to my creations. I use what I have, when I have it, and when I feel like it. Don't misunderstand; I don't bake. Cakes, pies, cookies, fancy breads, any baked items: all these are meant to be enjoyed outside of my own house, at restaurants, or coffee houses, or at a friend's home. When I compliment those, for sure I won't accept any recipes, and I agree those items probably need strict adherence to recipe rules. Chemistry and all. So, no thanks, seriously, baking is not my thing.

I'm a little more confused when people ask me for one of my recipes. Honestly, I can't give an answer since I didn't really follow a recipe! And I'm not lying to protect any kind of copyright, either, although people wonder. I do get suspicious glares.

Of course, many will disagree with my methods. That's okay. Food is personal. However, I have decided to share some of my own recipe stories. Copy and try them…if you dare.

Hamburger Soup

Once I became a working mother, like the rest of us super-moms of the 1980s and '90s, I was charged (self-appointed) with the feeding and caring of a family of active boys. Two were children who needed lots of healthful feeding and watering to grow big and strong, and one was a husband already big and strong enough, who needed to stop the growing of the middle-aged spread. I will admit that I myself needed to watch by that age, too. Why didn't we bottle that magical teenaged metabolism when we had the chance?

Meals had to be filling and fast and as full of nutrients as I could conjure. A routine began after work and school, knapsacks and gym bags crashed and dropped on top of hundreds (seemed like) pairs of shoes and boots around the entrance hall of our PMQ in Cold Lake, Alberta.

"Mom, what's for dinner?" This would be D'Arcy, my six-year-old.

Husband Don would chime in, "I'll make it, but you have to tell me what."

Me, to any of them: "Don't have a sandwich now! Supper's coming in 20 minutes."

From my three-year-old, Sasha, "I'm hungry! Pick me up! I have to pee."

Fortunately, as a second boy, Sasha could trundle off by then to make a mess around the toilet himself.

"Don, I'll set things out while you change, okay? D'Arcy, no crackers! Go set the table. Then you can watch TV."

"Well, what are we having? Plates or bowls?"

Back to me. *Hopefully we had something we can use from the night before,* I'm thinking as I open the fridge. *Yay, leftover mashed potatoes. No meat, though.*

I open the freezer and find a package of ground beef. Thank goodness for microwaves, the supermom appliance of my life. I put the frozen lump in for a few minutes, then check out the cupboard for appropriate cans of food. Good, there's vegetable or vegetable beef and barley soup in here. Vegetable is fine for tonight, since I've got the ground beef. One can might not be enough for all of us, though. Add a can of chopped tomatoes. Bought a case of them on sale in Lloydminster at the new warehouse-style Superstore there last month. All I need now is something green. Any kind of which is in my wonderful freezer of course.

"D'Arcy, peas or spinach?"

"Peas!"

Good, spinach only comes in blocks in these years, hard to chop out. "Okay. Put bowls and spoons on the table. Can you pour the milk? Dad wants water. And put bread and butter on, too. Or crackers if you want."

And then Don comes back. I show him the ingredients, and he takes over while I go change out of work clothes. The microwave dings.

And somehow, like the opening scene out of *The Simpsons*, we all assemble at the dinner table as Don brings out the steaming pot of supper.

My grandmother visited us once in Cold Lake. She was in her late eighties and had raised six children of her own on the farm. I served her some of my leftover soup.

"My, this is the best hamburger soup I've ever had. You'll have to give me the recipe."

When I told her it was just ground beef with canned and frozen and leftover ingredients added, like I mentioned, I don't think she thought I was telling the truth. How could I not know what the result would be; how could I not have a recipe to give her? How could I be serious? But I was. And she did give me a name for this (albeit mercurial) dish. It's my Hamburger Soup recipe.

I'd give you the recipe, but I think this story speaks for itself.

Family Mush

The one meal that defines my cooking style, created for feeding my own family, is affectionately called "mush." The soup version you've already encountered. Here follows more about the stew-type version.

First, there's a starchy filler base to build upon. It can be rice, potatoes, or pasta, but not often potato. That one will be called shepherd's pie, or like my Québecois boys would say, *pâté chinois*. (That had been confusing to this Anglophone immigrant. The first time I heard the term was when watching a French sitcom that my son was laughing at. The family in the show were eating *pâté chinois*, and I thought they had ordered Chinese food.)

So, the rice should be the firmer, parboiled kind, not white Minute rice (the newer brown Minute rice seems fine) nor jasmine nor anything delicate. It can be made up first, while you get the cans and other ingredients ready. If doing the pasta base, true mush won't include spaghetti, because if you use spaghetti, then that meal is called spaghetti and not mush. Use the fusilli or bows or plain old macaroni if you're making mush.

In homage to the macaroni: Thank you Kraft dinner. You've been a part of my life from earliest times to my lactose-free homemade mush versions.

My mother baked macaroni and cheese with crumbs on top that still can't be beat, especially in memory, but once those boxes with the cheese powder hit the shelves in my early childhood, it was a staple. I've been making KD since I could read. I made it for my own children, too, and taught them the same lesson: if you can read, you can cook, just follow the instructions printed on the box.

Back to the mush. It has to include a protein. Sometimes beans (especially with the tomato kind, in which case it could become a chili), but usually a ground meat. We liked ground pork when the kids were young because it was tastier and cheaper, but today my favourite is a mix of ground beef and pork together. Leftover beef, ham, or pork chops can also be used, but you must cut it up into biteable chunks.

There are three versions of the sauce to mix with the rice or pasta: the cheese-y (again, thanks to KD, the original), the creamy, and the tomato-y.

Does anyone remember Richard Simmons, the fitness TV phenom of the 1980s? I watched his frenetic show; the energy was contagious. Less well-known was his diet advice, or as he called it, his "live-it" advice. It consisted of colour-coding your meals with playing cards. Deal a set of cards for your meal, the goal being to make as colourful a set as possible. That resonated with me and still does—colour your meals colourful! So, even if the mush begins as beige or yellow or white with the brown of the meat, it must contain as much colour as you can toss in.

The orange KD (Is it still as orange as when artificial colours were allowed?) pairs well with frozen peas or frozen spinach, nice and bright green. The tomato-based mushes are good with mushrooms (fresh if you have time, canned are okay if not) and again, frozen spinach.

Creamy versions are made with creamed soups, especially cream of mushroom, but also cream of celery is popular. These creamy mushes also take well to frozen peas, and chopped up carrots really pop. The mashed potatoes in the shepherd's pie includes frozen corn of course, but I always add peas, too.

You can see these meals were cheap, healthy, fast, and easy. I give a special shout-out to canned soups and frozen vegetables, civilization's greatest food contributions, in my humble opinion. But as happens, eventually, the kids grow up, big and strong, and leave home. Don and I got richer, had more time, and my "mushes" became a thing of the past. More expensive cuts of meat entered our meals, too much rich red cuts, frankly, of beef ribs and steaks and pork tenderloin. Fresher versions of exotic vegetables were purchased, things like Swiss chard and golden beets—meals became longer to prepare and more expensive to assemble. And despite my continued insistence on green things, those western middle-aged health concerns began to assert themselves: weight gain, higher cholesterol levels, even gout. So, it's back to basics again in our retirement years.

Now we can make "gourmet" versions of my early family mushes, with fancier cheeses (lactose-free), and chopped steak or lean ground beef. Mushes require much less red meat per serving, healthier for us both. I can add onions and red peppers now (which the kids didn't like) to the colourful mix, or even mince up those new leafy greens, things my kids wouldn't eat or that were too fussy to prepare in working mom years.

Don and I don't make mushes as often for just the two of us, but when the kids come home to visit, I'll often make a pot of memorable ingredients, simple with the throwback frozen peas and corn, and despite them being in their thirties with their own jobs and families to feed, they'll still say, "Yay, mush! Pass the parmesan!"

Then we have some expensive dessert from the French bakery and perhaps some fine wine or coffee with Bailey's.

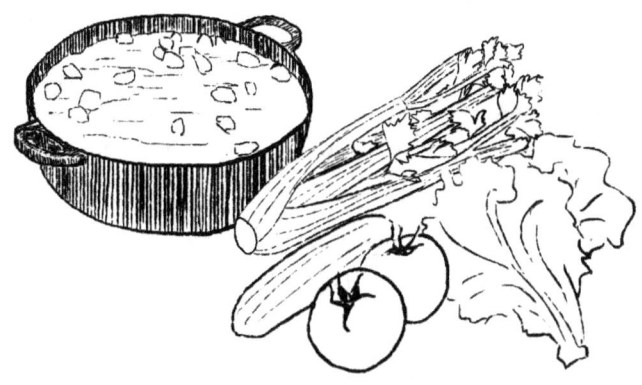

Snack Nachos

Everyone knows how to make nachos—put cheese on tortilla chips and melt in the microwave. Ah, but the variations are limitless! Here's how I made the best ones ever:

Ingredients

- Lime-flavoured Tostitos chips
- Lactose-free cheeses, preferably one white, one orange. Use old cheddar, or better yet, very old. Never any "light" variety; it won't melt properly.
- Salsa, store brand of your choice. I like medium hot.
- Frozen corn
- Guacamole, store brand of your choice **or** fresh avocado **or** both

Method

1. Lay the tortilla chips on a dinner plate. Don't overlap them.
2. Slice the cheese and make sure each chip has some placed on it. You'll miss some anyway, but we'll deal with those cheese-less ones at the end.
3. Make the dip separately in a cereal-sized bowl. Start by dumping a handful of the frozen corn in, microwave it.
4. Add the salsa and slice up the avocado or scoop the guacamole in. Mush it all up together, then microwave again until hot, not bubbling.
5. While the dip cools, microwave the chips and cheese.

6. All is ready. Use a spoon for each piece of chips with melted cheese. Enjoy!
7. We're not done: after all the chips with cheese are eaten, there are crumbs of cheese-less chips and some dip left over. Crush up those leftover chips and dump into the dip bowl. Use your spoon and eat it all up. Nacho salad.

The best versions of this I ever made involved adding extra red onions and red peppers, and for the chips, I found guacamole-flavoured chips in the health food store to mix in with the regular lime-flavoured ones. That masterpiece hasn't been repeated. The real trick to these snack nachos is to limit the quantities so that nothing is overpowering. Good luck, as all the ingredients invite overdoing.

Salads

Salads are a big meal staple with me. I have three kinds that I make: lunch salads, supper salads, and side salads. All of them are not hard to put together, but they are time-consuming, which I guess makes them difficult? Your call.

Lunch Salad

"Janna, I'm leaving for work now. What time do you have to get up?"

My daughter-in-law—tall, young, with flowing brunette hair that clogged up the vacuum cleaner for months after any visit, much like the blond hair of my eldest son's wife—comes yawning out of our spare bedroom in our retirement condo in Aylmer, Québec. Well, eventually it would be our retirement condo. Sometimes life has alternate plans. My son Sasha had returned to use that spare bedroom a couple of times for months on end while he sorted out his own life's path. Don had fully retired by now, but I found myself still working to keep busy and to keep the retirement funds where we needed them to be. Frankly, I didn't hate my job, especially at only three days a week, and didn't want to hang around the condo all day kicking young people out of bed.

But things were looking up. Sasha had recently left his furniture store job, where he'd met Janna, to join the military. He was away now on training before he would get his first posting, along to which he planned to take his "Québec wife" Janna. By Québec wife, I mean that like most young Québec couples, they would live common-law, as in together as husband and wife, but not officially married with a certificate. Hey, not my culture, but my kids did grow up in Québec. Like immigrants everywhere, I'm not a fan of everything in my new world but have to accept what I cannot change. I still had hopes for an eventual "real" wedding for them. My older son D'Arcy and Jessica were "really" married, after all. Meanwhile Janna, while she technically still lived at home with her parents in rural Dunrobin, across the river in Ontario, was spending weekday nights with us in Aylmer to take advantage of better bus access to her university classes in Ottawa. We didn't mind; she was a daughter that I'd always wished for! She liked watching nighttime TV with us until our early bedtime, after which, like most young people, she would stay up to do whatever screen things young people did these days. Facebook, texting, homework? Maybe. She did introduce me to the freaktastic TV series *American Horror Story*, to my delight and Don's uncomfortable acceptance.

"Janna, I made extra lunch salad. Will you take some to school today?"

Janna confounded me about food. Unlike my boys, I couldn't pin down what she liked, or didn't like, or would eat, or wouldn't. She wouldn't eat dairy, she was allergic. But she loved lattes and ice cream. She wasn't hungry, she didn't eat any supper. She was ravenous and ate candy all night from bulk-store bags. Peaches made her break out, I think, or was that the allergy? She shopped at the Chinese grocery store and bought mounds of leafy things I couldn't identify or cook, and they'd stay in the crisper until they went wilty and brown. She liked buying in bulk, but not really cooking in bulk. I was quite confused. *Is this normal with girls?* I wondered.

But I figured out she might like my work lunch salad of pasta with chopped up veggies and faux crab chunks. She watched me make it the night before, to her amusement, which I didn't understand.

"You're making lunch for tomorrow, tonight? That's funny," she said. I didn't get the joke. But on a hunch, I made enough for two, and put them in separate Tupperware dishes, and taped plastic forks to the lids on top and put them in the fridge. "Yes, for tomorrow," I said.

And surprise! Janna did take the lunch salad. She crammed it sideways down into her overstuffed daypack (hence the taped fork) that morning for school. And I even think she ate it, although who really knows. The Tupperware came back empty, the fork lost somewhere along in the day.

I am fully retired now, and Janna and Sasha live far away on their first military posting in Edmonton, Alberta. I still have to "work" sometimes for a day; I will have a writing workshop or a book signing to attend, where I might need to bring my own lunch. And if I mention that to Janna on the phone, she'll laugh and ask if I'm making my pasta salad the night before to take. I still don't understand why she thinks it's so funny, but I don't mind or care.

Here's my work lunch salad recipe. Somewhat fussy to make, so I do it the night before. Also, the salad dressing soaks in better overnight—it tastes better made the night before. Besides, you wouldn't have time to make it for a workday on the same morning!

Ingredients

- Fusilli pasta (or bows, or plain macaroni in a pinch)
- Faux crab, sticks or chunks
- Frozen corn
- Fresh veggies, whatever you have, aim for colour: celery, radish, onion, peppers

Method

1. Get the pasta going. I'm not explaining how to boil water here!
2. Microwave the corn.
3. Wash and chop up the veggies, cut them into smaller than bite-sized chunks.
4. As soon as the pasta is *al dente*, rinse it in cold water to stop it from getting mushy.
5. In the container you want to save the salad in (I use a Tupperware sandwich container with a lid), dump in the pasta and all the veggies
6. Cut up the faux crab into the mix.
7. Douse with your favourite salad dressing. I use a vinegary one like Italian. You know by now I can't do creamy (the milk thing).

Taping the fork to the lid, plastic or otherwise, works well. Nothing worse than forgetting the cutlery and slurping your pasta with your fingers the next day.

Supper Salad

Sometimes I need a light supper. Maybe I already had lupper or a larger-than-usual lunch. For example, I could have had breakfast (yogurt and fruit), second breakfast (egg, toast, and coffee), a glass of wine after a curling game (other team paid as I lost the game), a cold pasta "salad" at a cafeteria (no veggies in it to speak of), then an afternoon snack of tea, nuts, and chocolate. It's now later than usual for suppertime; I'm tired and not especially hungry. I didn't eat any veggies, much less anything green today. What to do? Supper salad!

Here's the recipe. It's healthy, yes, like I always try with my meals, but also easy and fast, which is not my normal style but the exception that proves my rule.

Ingredients

- Lettuce: preferably leaf or romaine, with some butter (Boston) lettuce added if you have it. Never iceberg lettuce; how is that tasteless stuff even considered a food?
- Other veggies as available or as you feel like preparing. Sometimes I just microwave frozen peas and corn to toss on the lettuce. Sometimes I only use lettuce.
- Boneless chicken, like thighs, but of course the standard breast meat works. Actually, any meat that you have around that you can cook will work. Pork chop. Frozen meatballs. Fish sticks.
- Salad dressing of your choice.

Instructions

1. Cook the meat. Fry or bake or microwave. Nothing needs to be added but add sauce as desired; you know how to cook whatever meat you choose.
2. Cut up the lettuce directly onto plates. I haven't mentioned this yet, but I like my lettuce and veggies cut up small. It's so annoying when a whole leaf has to be crammed into your mouth, salad dressing smearing on your face, like many restaurants serve it.

3. Add the other veggies, if you felt like getting them ready.
4. Add the cooked meat, precut to bite-sized chunks.
5. Apply your favourite salad dressing.
6. Pour another glass of white wine (Did you miss the first one?) and enjoy.

Side Salad: Coleslaw

I use this term for the shredded cabbage salad. First, I must mention the etymology of coleslaw because I love word origins and I never knew where the name came from until I researched it for this story. It derives from two Dutch words: *kool*, meaning cabbage and *sla*, a shortened form of salad morphed by English into "slaw." So, coleslaw literally means cabbage salad. Of course, coming from English ancestors, I've also heard it called "cold slaw," which is a term also still in use. I've noticed that coleslaw is not really in style with the younger generation, who've only heard of it as a side with fish and chips in restaurant meals. Most restaurant coleslaw doesn't deserve to be considered edible. It's too runny, hard, vinegary, or it's served in a tiny paper cup that turned it into a simple garnish. This is too bad, as fresh coleslaw is a delicious, cheap, and super-healthy food choice. For those who know better, make it again! For those who don't, try it, you'll like it!

I have three versions of coleslaw, good and quick, better and not-so-quick, and best and not quick at all.

Simplest Version

The good and quick is the one you buy pre-packaged. It is good enough and remarkably cheap. Just add your own dressing.

Some tips:

- After dumping into a large bowl, sift it around and pick out the large, hard, unpalatable chunks of cabbage that the mechanical processing will leave in.
- The packaged stuff can be dry, especially if you bought it on sale because it's getting old. Add a few sprinkles of water before the dressing and toss it around. Don't drench it, but freshen up the old cabbage; it will come around a bit.
- Your dressing is your choice. I've used ready-made, of every kind, but I always add a capful of vinegar, to further make it pop. Most creamy style ready-made dressings are too bland. The vinegar addition perks it up.

The simplest dressing is just mayonnaise plus vinegar. Creamy and perky.

Tip on the dressing: Don't overdo. Too much and it will be runny later. Let the salad sit for at least a couple of hours before serving; the vinegar will soften and settle down the cabbage. Add more dressing after those couple of hours if needed, but surprisingly, it seldom does.

Now, I rarely do this simple version, because it's never too much trouble to do the better version.

Better Version

Prepare with pre-packaged coleslaw, then make the following additions. They will juice up the cabbage nicely.

1. Shred your own extra carrot, fresh from your own fridge, into the pre-packaged mix. Not cut-up chunks; use your metal grater or food processor.
2. Chop up some onion, if you have the time. Don't grate the onion.
3. Even better, chop up an apple, with or without skin. I like it chopped into the smallest chunks possible, but don't try to shred an apple, either. And don't add the apple without the carrot. They go together.
4. Add the dressing as in the *Simple version*.

Best Version

Finally, the best coleslaw is the same as the *Better Version* with the major exception of the cabbage. It is not pre-packaged; you've shredded it yourself. Fresh and juicy, but time-consuming. Again, your call.

Grilled Cheese

The summer I turned twelve was a traumatizing one. Nothing tragic happened, but my father was transferred to a tiny radar station near Yorkton, Saskatchewan, in the middle of the Canadian prairies. We'd just spent two years in Goose Bay, Labrador, and I'd loved it there. It might as well have been a transfer to another planet for all the difference between the two locations. Goose Bay, fresh northern tundra to hot dry farmland. It was hot in the summer; winters would prove as bitter as any cold day in Labrador. From life at a big Canadian air base, with an even bigger American B-52 bomber base, plus British base, to a tiny little station of only 90 PMQs and a 10-kilometer (might as well have been 100 miles) drive to the small prairie city of Yorkton. It was dizzying.

Even more traumatizing than the shocking change of scenery and culture was the introduction to my prairie relatives. Both my parents were from big family, small town Manitoba, nearby to Saskatchewan and certainly of the same farm culture. My parents were thrilled to be "home," but of course, I didn't know what being home felt like at twelve years old, having lived in Kingston, Calgary, Germany, Labrador, and now Saskatchewan. So the burgeoning amateur anthropologist that I was pretending to become, I proceeded to observe. As usual, I had to learn many new things on this posting, food being of course part of such learning. As in this story.

"You've never had mustard on your grilled cheese? Weird."

My cousin, Wendy, a year older at thirteen, and I were fending for ourselves. Parents were out at the mess, and my brothers? Who knew where they scampered off to when left under my lackadaisical babysitting care.

"Mustard on grilled cheese? No, never. No onions either, what are you doing?"

"You not only talk funny, but you can't be serious that you've never eaten a grilled cheese like this! Pass the eggs, we'll scramble them while the frying pan is still hot."

Well, my Newfoundlander accent from Goose Bay was fading, so this hurt a little. But the grilled cheese was nothing compared to what I saw next.

"Holy crap! What's in the egg yolk?" I screamed as she broke the shells over the side of the pan and dumped the raw egg in.

"Hey, look, it was a fertilized egg! Cool, you can see the little legs and everything. Look!" But I was not looking; I was horrified enough that I'd seen the blood streaks sizzling away already.

"Dump it out, I'm not eating that!"

And to be fair, Wendy wasn't going to either. But she sure laughed at my reaction. Until farmland Saskatchewan, I'd never thought about eggs being fertilized or not before we ate them. I still hold my breath when cracking eggs today.

As for grilled cheese with mustard and onion, well, that turned out to be delicious. In fact, over the years I got away from plain white bread and process cheese slices (no wonder it needed mustard and onions) to better, whole grain bakery breads, with real cheddar slices. And sharp, red onion, sliced thin enough to cook through. The best mustard is still good old yellow French's. The fancy ones aren't vinegary enough.

But the real secret to how I make my grilled cheese sandwiches today is not the ingredients. It's how difficult I make the process to achieve perfection. I use nothing short of three appliances. Timing and constant attention are also important. You know how you read cookbooks or take advice and recipes from friends that are always billed as "fast and easy?" Well, here is my recipe for a "time-consuming and fussy" grilled cheese sandwich.

Ingredients

- 2 slices of firm, not soft bread, something whole grain
- Butter (as much as needed, see Method)
- Real, old cheddar
- Fresh tomato
- Red onion
- French's yellow mustard

Required equipment

- Stovetop burner
- Frying pan: non-stick best but not really required if you use enough butter
- Toaster
- Paper towel
- Plate (microwaveable)
- Microwave
- Sharp knife for cutting tomatoes and/or onions
- Butter knife
- Egg Flipper (some people call this a spatula)

Method

Tip: Make sure you are the only person working in the kitchen. You'll need to dance around between appliances and use a lot of counter space.

1. Pop the bread in the toaster, just to crisp it up, not toast completely.
2. Turn on the stove and scoop a slab of butter in the pan.
3. Keep an eye on the butter, don't let it burn, just melt. Turn off the burner if you must.
4. Butter the bread, lightly, which is now warm enough to melt what you spread on.
5. Circle squirt the mustard on one (it's enough) buttered slice of bread.
6. If you pre-sliced the cheese, great, but if not, no worries. It doesn't matter now if the bread gets cold. Slice the cheese (a checkerboard pattern with white and orange cheddar is fun) on top of the mustard. Not too thick, not double layers.
7. Now, slice the tomato and/or onion slices on top of the cheese. I can't stress the importance of slicing as thinly as possible, but you may layer a little for these ingredients. Hope your knife is sharp enough.
8. You are ready to plop the second piece of buttered bread on top of the first, which is beautifully loaded up now. Press gently together, don't squish.
9. Lift your sandwich—be gentle, use two hands—and place on paper towel on the plate to place in the microwave. Don't forget the paper towel. It keeps the bread from getting soggy.
10. After microwaving (No more than 30 seconds, but as usual, microwaves vary, right?), if the bread is glued

together with the melted cheese, it is good. If the cheese is running out the sides, it was too long in the microwave, or you may have used too much cheese, a forgivable mistake.
11. While the sandwich is still warm from the microwave, gently butter the outside of one side of it.
12. Back to the frying pan. Place the sandwich, unbuttered side down, in the perfectly melted pool of butter in the frying pan.
13. Grab the egg flipper, gently prodding and sliding the sandwich around.
14. Just before the smoking starts (I know, how do you know when something is about to happen?), carefully flip over the sandwich to the previously buttered side.
15. Repeat the prodding, sliding, shaking, and moving around.
16. If the first side was a perfect golden brown, great. If not, repeat flipping and prodding.
17. No squishing. No squishing the sandwich, ever!
18. During a waiting time for the golden brown, fold the other half of the paper towel and replace the one used in the microwave on the plate.
19. Once both sides are golden, crispy brown, place back on the paper towel, on the plate.
20. During a different waiting time, or in advance, pour yourself a glass of milk.
21. Use that sharp knife to cut your perfectly grilled cheese sandwich in half. Notice the blend of melted ooze.
22. Enjoy, quickly, don't let it get cold. But be careful, don't burn your mouth with the hot tomato.

See? Fussy, a pain to prepare, lots of cleanup. But really, the best grilled cheese sandwich you'll every taste. Go ahead, see if I'm lying.

Spices

Do you have a spice rack? A spice drawer? A spice cupboard? I do and don't. Spices and I have an on/off relationship. I don't bake. But I do like to flavour my mushes and soups and salads and stir-fry dishes. I recently checked my cupboards where a spice jar or tin or bag might get placed. I was surprised at the collection being no less than twenty-six types of seasonings, containing what I collectively call spices: flakes of plants, scrapings of plant barks, or ground dried bits of flora.

I placed them on the counter together. When and where had such an assortment been acquired? Most were brand-named; seems Club House has been in my own house for decades. Here's my list in no particular order (just like I found them spread around my shelves in multiple cupboards), and what I remember about each.

Cinnamon. I love this word. Back in my IT days, I would assign this word as a default original password for clients I didn't like because it was always a challenge to spell. I bet it encouraged them to change it right away like they were supposed to. This is a spice that I use almost daily, at least on days when I make my gourmet oatmeal (refer to Breakfast chapter). I obviously buy it more regularly than other spices since I found a tin, a larger jar, and even some cinnamon sticks in a plastic box. I do remember buying these for Christmas grog drinks, but had forgotten they were still buried in the recesses of the shelves. They look like little ancient scrolls, which makes sense, as cinnamon is simply inner bark scrapings from a tree. I'm tempted to unroll them, but when I try, they just crack and crumble.

Curry. I went through a curry phase with stir fries and rice. Now that I've seen this again, I think I have a craving.

Mustard. I don't know why I have powdered mustard. We always use prepared mustard. In fact, my husband is a mustard fanatic, so maybe he bought it.

Turmeric. I think I bought this because somebody told me it was just like saffron, and I couldn't find saffron. I think I wanted saffron because somebody told me it was delicious on rice, and it was the most expensive spice you could buy. I use turmeric now to colour up my coleslaw, if I remember. It's the most wonderful rich gold.

Nutmeg. Used with cinnamon for my gourmet oatmeal, of course.

Allspice. I seriously thought this included a bunch of different spices mixed together to make all of them. In checking the ingredients, however, it only listed allspice, so I had to research this. Turns out, allspice is made from the berries of a plant, and is its own single ingredient. Again, an oatmeal flavouring.

Garlic powder. This one's easy. I buy it regularly and use it on anything. Spaghetti sauces and mashed potatoes for the daughters-in-law come to mind.

Oregano. One of the spices I need when making my own dressing for turkey dinners.

Paprika. My mother always put this in devilled eggs, but I don't know why I have it. Now that I know, I can imagine several uses for its punch and rich rusty red colour.

White pepper. Why?

Black peppercorns. Because we still have a peppermill to put on the table for fancy meals or company.

Parsley. I like sprinkling this on things that need the colour green added throughout. Nothing comes to mind, but I must use it somewhere, sometimes, don't I?

Thyme. Another one for the turkey dressing, but sometimes on salads, if I remember.

Vanilla extract. I didn't know I had any of this and can't remember why I do. I know it is used in many baking recipes, but I don't bake, so... Sometimes I imagine that my mother has visited and put such things in my kitchen. I can picture her as she opens the cupboard door and stands there, inhaling all the scents softly exuding from the shelves, pausing and closing her eyes to better enjoy the aromas of years of unsorted spices stashed around boxes of pasta and cans of soup. Then, I hear her voice: "What? No vanilla? How do you get by without any vanilla?"

Then there are the spice mixtures pre-combined and ready-made:

Roasted garlic and peppers. A favourite. To be used in spaghetti sauce, pasta salad, or on rice.

Poultry seasoning: sage, thyme, coriander, marjoram. I use this one in the dressings I make when stuffing a turkey. Again, awesome words with fascinating origins. I can understand why I didn't buy each spice separately though, what with making dressing so rarely these days. I wonder how long ago I bought this one. It's a local store brand, so within the last 25 years is my best guess. I wonder if these spice things have expiry dates, then realize that of course they do. I really must check and toss. Someday.

Cider spices. Lots of sugar. They're meant for adding to warmed-up red wine. Christmas smells like this.

Spicy pepper medley. I thought it was my roasted garlic and peppers and bought it by mistake. Spicy. It's good on steak.

Lemon and herb and lemon pepper. These are billed as salt-substitutes, which isn't true as nothing compares to salt. They're okay in place of salt, but even better with salt added. I try on and off to go off of salt.

Thai one-step seasoning. I must have foolishly thought at one time while browsing the spices in the grocery store, *Oh, Thai seasoning, this is all I need to cook Thai food myself at home!* And so, I bought this one. I won't bore you with the list of ingredients, but I counted them: 23! Some sounded normal and yummy, like cilantro and lime juice powder. Others are listed by their chemical compound names. One is simply listed as "flavour," which is interesting because the label in front advertises "No artificial colours or flavours." I guess the flavour ingredient is real, not fake, whatever it is.

Caesar rim spice. You'll be forgiven if you skip over this list of ingredients. I myself enjoy (maybe that's a strong word) reading labels, so here goes. This spice jar contains salt, red pepper, sugar, citric acid, corn maltodextrin, onion powder, and again, that magical ingredient, "flavour." I bought this specifically to make the famous Canadian cocktail, the Caesar.

Caesar cocktail

Here's how I learned how to make a Caesar. It's pretty basic compared to the variations in restaurants nowadays; most of them could be considered complete meals with their additions of pickled string beans and bacon.

Ingredients and method

Using a tall glass, add, in order:
1. Ice cubes
2. Vodka
3. Clamato juice
4. Horseradish
5. Stick of celery, use for stirring, then munch it
6. Sprinkle in the Caesar spice mix and use the celery stick to stir it all up.

You can pre-wet the rim of the glass, even better with lemon juices, and dip it in the Caesar spice mix before adding all the drink ingredients, like a pro, but honestly, that's a lot of fuss and mess, and I always forget before adding the liquids to the glass anyway. My way still works.

My Rules

Many would agree, especially in my own patriarchal society, that our mothers and other women have been responsible for preparing the food, or at least planning for its home consumption. I provide the ideas for, if not always all the work of, delivering our meals. Stirring, frying, timing: I often leave this grunt work to the *sous-chef*, my husband. I am especially in charge of food for any visiting family or company. I understand not all families or cultures are like mine; it's just how it is in our household. If left to my husband, all we'd eat would be chicken wings, bacon, pizza, and take-out. There are some who would agree that this would be a wonderful way to live, but in my experience, it is not a long-term strategy for any kind of health.

You live, you learn, you try to make things better for yourself, your children, your community, your world. As the woman of the family, it was and is my (self-appointed) job to pass on what food culture I feel still serves a need. So, here is a list of traditions I would like to pass along. They will be used (or tossed away) as will fit the reader and the changes each generation makes to culture. Food will always serve a need. How, when, and what we eat are the variables that change. I hope the next generation finds some of my advice useful. If not, well, it's up to them to modify things for themselves and their own children.

Here's my own sage advice:

Never eat in the car. Unless it's a road trip, and then you may eat road trip food, such as can be purchased at gas stations: nuts, meat jerky, pop, coffee and chocolate. Sometimes potato chips. I can imagine this advice not making the cut for cultural continuity, as first, what are gas stations of the future, and second, what's meat jerky? Both gas and meat do not look to have a foreseeable future.

Never eat standing up, always eat while sitting, preferably at a table, and in the company of others. This one, also, seems destined for oblivion, as "others" has come to mean one's handheld connection to people on the internet.

Always eat something for breakfast before you leave the house in the morning. It's called breakfast for a reason. It breaks the fast of your hours of sleeping time. I still follow this one, but it was hard for my own children. I don't know why, because when I was still in charge of their eating, they always ate a good breakfast. Come the teen years, however, they preferred the five extra minutes of sleep to the toast and juice that time would have taken to prepare, so I came up with ideas for them.

I cannot vouch for their adherence today as adults, but here they are:

Toast to go. With peanut butter if possible, although during my own food-preparing mom years, peanut butter would become forbidden in schools. Cheese then. Even processed slices. We must adapt.

Banana. Nature's perfect snack food, package included.

Breakfast milk drinks like instant powdered ones. These would evolve into the ready-made ones in plastic bottles, like Boost. In fact, if not for Boost, my younger son might never have kept his weight up during his growing teen years for his sports, as he didn't like to eat before hockey games, nor afterwards, except for chocolate milk or Boost. Today? I think the after-hockey beer (or as Don Cherry would say, "pop") keeps the weight up just fine for those rec league players.

Granola bars. Too much sugar, especially when they first came out, but of course one cannot argue their pre-packaged convenience and longevity. A case in the back cupboard will help get you through any downfall of civilization. I imagine they could be bartered at that time for other necessities. I've inherited some prepping tendencies from pioneer ancestors.

Eat something green every day. Again, being used to boys my whole life who don't think of salads as a food, this is a challenge I've mastered and follow for myself, but I'm not sure yet if it has been passed along. We'll see. When I have company, I always put out some variation of a salad, plus two cooked vegetables, one of which must be green. Frozen spinach balls work in a number of recipes, like mashed into potatoes or into any kind of soup. I don't think I've ever just served spinach as plain spinach, though. Although I do with Swiss chard, which is similar. Don't ask me why.

Go for rainbows with your meals. They need a variety of colour. With the green thing, add orange or red or yellow. In my house, there is always a brown (the meat) and usually a white (potatoes or rice), so the colour has to come from the vegetables. Fresh carrots mixed with broccoli is a standard, with another side of frozen corn. Or coleslaw. (Refer to 'Recipe Chapter-Sort of' for my coleslaw recipe.)

Don't eat after supper. This one is nearly impossible to follow, but it's the only advice I have for keeping one's weight under control, and the only dieting rule I've ever found effective. Good luck with this one.

Create your own family food culture and traditions. We always eat dessert (if we are having dessert) after dishes cleanup, for example. Another: I mash carrots into mashed potatoes. I try to always serve my mashed concoctions when my daughters-in-law are in attendance. Young women love carbs. The boys insist on lots of meat, however, something

I try to curb, for them, for their own good, after all. Again, good luck.

Best Meals of my Life

There are meals and food you can recall as either fantastic or otherwise, but they aren't always the ones you think they would be. For example, I cannot remember what I ate at my own wedding. The cake, sure, because of the pictures. It was a fruitcake, like Queen Victoria had, with butter icing, and cut into little finger-sized rectangles wrapped in white lacey paper doilies tied with ribbon to be handed out to guests. But the meal? Did I even pick out the menu?

I'm pretty sure that was something my mother did, being only eighteen myself at the time. You'd think that such an important day would stand out more in memory, but perhaps it was because the occasion was so momentous, trivial details like the meal are forgotten.

Then again, memory is a funny thing. Why do I remember what I ate the day my mother passed away? With no appetite that morning at the Health Sciences Centre, in a hurry to get back to her bedside for final goodbyes, I grabbed from the cafeteria a whole, juicy, mid-July ripe-red Manitoba tomato to take with me. A basket of them sat fresh on the counter by the cashier, free for the taking, brought in by someone from their lush Winnipeg home garden. As I sat with my father and brothers and family that morning, an unusual daytime thunderstorm breaking and crashing lightning outside the high windows in our private family grieving area, I bit into that tomato. I can taste it still, rich and full of summer. As my mother gracefully slipped away from her own life, I sucked and licked that juicy fruit with all the gratitude for my mother's gifts that I could. Words cannot express grief like that, but the memory of that tomato stays with me always.

Here are other memorable moments of eating to share.

First Anniversary

I'm older now, and have been married for decades to my first, turns out only, husband, Don. We weren't always the upper-middle class folk we are today, who can afford a nice dinner out on our anniversary or anytime at all. Because we were just teenagers at our wedding in Petawawa in 1976, the date (and indeed everything) was chosen and planned by my mother, with no objections at all from me. I'd never even heard the term "bridezilla" in 1976, much less knew enough about how to act like one. So, my wedding occurred on a Saturday, on October 30. Now, try to think back to 1976. Or look it up in a history book. Life was more traditional, as in, even though we didn't practice it "religiously," my mother's and my own Anglican religion played a part in my wedding. I had an afternoon church wedding, followed by a reception at my father's Sergeant's mess. As I said, it was a Saturday. October 30. The mess was booked that night after my wedding reception for a huge Hallowe'en party. We arrived at the 2:00 p.m reception hall to decorations of witches and black cats and, as my mother said, "Other pagan things not appropriate for a wedding," plastered everywhere. She was horrified and ran around tearing them down. But Don and I didn't care, and I have a wedding picture of our first dance with a grinning cardboard skeleton in the background on the wall behind us.

Fast forward to our first wedding anniversary. What a whirlwind year we'd had. We moved right away to Brantford, where Don had followed his parents to get a job in a store to support his new wife and life. Which didn't work out long past the winter. By spring, he'd applied to join the military; by summer, he'd done his basic training; and by fall, he was on his trades training in Winnipeg where I'd joined him by living with an aunt. It's now October 30th, and we're in Winnipeg, Manitoba. We're very poor—unqualified privates were not paid a living wage in 1977, and I was only a part-time lifeguard and student at the University of Winnipeg—but we don't mind as we don't have many financial obligations... yet. Don's still in barracks and I'm living with a relative who doesn't charge me very much for the room. But being our first wedding anniversary, and in what would become our tradition, we decide to go out for a celebratory dinner. We headed downtown. Again, look up in your history book about downtown Winnipeg in 1977. There was no touristy district that I recall, or could afford. The Forks (look up how touristy Winnipeg is today) wouldn't be a thing for decades. I know there were fancy restaurants, but nothing that we or our circle of friends, outsiders to Winnipeg as military folk are, knew anything about. My aunt and uncle had taken us to a neighbourhood Italian place once, but this was our first anniversary—shouldn't we find something more special?

How *did* we find something? I don't remember how. There was a downtown district we thought must be promising, so off we went and parked our rusty Chevy Vega. A Sunday night, the streets were deserted and quickly turning dark that time of year. We wandered along the sidewalks, looking for a restaurant, and noticed lights and noise coming from below down some stairs, with a small sign at street level pointing down, to The Underground Pizza Works. Cold and knowing we liked pizza, we entered.

It was like a warm, cozy cave inside, dark with a low ceiling but cheery with candlelight and very crowded. We were shown to a small side table by a costumed cat woman, or maybe she was a vampire. We looked around and all the staff and many of the customers were in costume, as witches or in heavy makeup. There was that fake spider web stuff hanging everywhere, and even dry ice misting in the corners of the room. A Hallowe'en party! Just like on our wedding day. Don and I ordered a beer and cocktail and awaited our pizza order, which turned out to be the best we'd ever eaten; Winnipeg, like Chicago, is famous for pizza. It was a thin crust, salted on the sides and bottom. Not overloaded with sauce or pepperoni or mushrooms, but just right. In the decades since that pizza, I've never had anything that came close, except maybe some wood-fired ones that approached its perfection, yet only enough to remind me of that first anniversary at the Underground Pizza Works. Perhaps it was the ambiance, our romantic first year, the Hallowe'en backdrop, but no matter, it was one of the most memorable meals of my life.

Years later, Don's military career had us posted back to Winnipeg. Of course we looked for the Underground Pizza Works again, but sadly, it was gone, and no one we asked had ever heard of it. I like to think it was a Twilight Zone episode for the two young newly-weds, searching and finding their perfect first anniversary meal. A special never-to-be-repeated kind of magic.

The Steak Stories

"Wow, I've never seen a woman eat like that."

Now, I know Jari meant this statement as a compliment, but at that moment, I paused the fork overflowing with New York cheesecake, cool and gelled just right, and set it back down on the oversized restaurant plate, drizzled with sauce, dappled with plump fruit—cherry, my favourite, not strawberry.

"What's that supposed to mean? Are you saying I'm a pig?" I could talk to Jari as to a brother. Brothers, with which I'd had many years of experience. One could even say, in the early years of my marriage to Don, before we had kids (More boys!), I missed my brothers and the kind of rough camaraderie I couldn't replicate with my college girlfriends. You couldn't call out a college girlfriend for hinting you were a pig, for example.

"No, no, you misunderstand, my dear!" Jari still had a slight Polish accent and spoke almost old-fashioned, using very correct English. He was about five years older than Don and me, a full sergeant when he was accepted at Royal Military College in Kingston, Ontario, in the same program as my young husband, who was away for his summer military trades training. Jari was our neighbour, and didn't need the same summer training, so was home. Newly separated from his wife and young son, he was lonely in the evenings, too, and had invited me out to supper. At a very nice restaurant, something like a Keg Steakhouse, although I can't remember the exact name. His treat, as his sergeant's pay was certainly better than Don's at corporal; my own income being zero during these student years.

"I simply meant, in my years of dating women, I've never had one order an appetizer before and dessert after a full steak dinner. I'm impressed, I meant no disrespect. Honestly. I'm impressed." By now, he was laughing.

I guess I could eat a lot in those days. I rode my bike to Queen's University from the base every day that summer; I still swam and went to the gym. And I was still young, baby fat gone and mother-to-be fat not yet built up. A restaurant steak dinner with loaded baked potato, escargot and cheesecake was not to be wasted. So, I didn't. Thanks, Jari!

Funny, I do recall that steak dinner as among

the best of my life, but it didn't compare to the first, best T-bone steak I ever ate. That one was when I was only 11 years old, living in Goose Bay, Labrador, and it certainly was not at a fancy restaurant.

As usual, the family was called to dinner after either I or my brothers had set the table in the separate dining room. (Whoever set the table didn't have to clear it, and dishes duty was also rostered.)

"Don't forget to put the good steak knives on, from the buffet drawer," my mother said as she sat down.

A wonderful aroma was coming from the kitchen, and Dad was saying, "Coming, just a minute!" I guess Dad was cooking something tonight.

Not cooking. We could hear the sizzling. Dad was frying. Frying steaks. He carried in a huge plate piled with perfectly charred meat, wafting steam as he set it on the table and sat at his seat, at the far end from Mom's, which was naturally nearest the kitchen. I don't know why, by the way, because if anything was ever needed from the kitchen during a meal, it was "Mickey, Mark, John, Jeffrey, someone! Go get *whatever!*"

Dad had a huge two-pronged fork and asked us to pass over our plates. The slab of T-bone filled my whole plate with no room at all for potatoes or vegetables.

"Don't worry, just eat the meat! This is the best steak you'll ever eat! Eat up kids! Anyone want HP sauce? Mickey, Mark, go get it from the kitchen." My mother was laughing and shaking her head. Really, six giant T-bones, even one for my littlest brother who was only four!

"Dig in!"

We dug in. It was juicy; greasy fat slathered all over our faces. I was getting full.

"Eat the meat around the bone, use your fingers, it's the best part." Dad was right. We kept up.

Cognac, the family dog, was in heaven, having perched himself underneath Jeffrey's seat. He didn't need to beg; we all had more than we could handle.

I wonder today where Dad got all those expensive, delicious steaks. In Goose Bay, it was kind of feast or famine at the base grocery store, very dependent in 1969 on what came in on the cargo planes and when. Mom could order stuff and then store cases of things like canned peaches or pineapple down in the unfinished basement of our PMQ, but we kids were adept with can openers and would gobble up such cases of treats well before the next shipment would come in.

Steaks? Beef T-bone steaks like we had that night, must have come in special order and cost a fortune, but Dad must have had a craving. Or, more likely, it was some trade that Dad was finagling with one of the military mess cooks. Whatever, however, it was the best steak of my life.

It must be said that now, in comfy middle-old-age, I don't eat steak at home at all. It's a restaurant food for me, where it can be cooked properly. I never matched my father's expertise of that Goose Bay experience. Funny that my favourite steaks now are at restaurants where they serve chunks of aged, tenderized prime cuts like tenderloin on something called a hot stone. The meat is raw as it arrives sizzling on this superheated lava stone. Served after a glass of red wine, and maybe another one, I've never burned myself on this serving stone. And as you cut each soft buttery slice of meat and roll it around to cooked perfection, then dip it both to cool it off and coat it in tangy, salty spicy sauce, you stop and admire your own fantastic steak, each bite as perfect as the first one.

The Best Appetizer

It's not always the most expensive foods that taste the best. Many memorable meals of my life are not about the type of food consumed at all, but the conditions around the consumption. I'm talking about the when and why we eat, not the what. I would wager that the best food in life is that which is earned by fresh air and hard work. Here's an example.

"I'm freezing. I hope the ball doesn't get hit out here in right field. I doubt I could catch it. I can't feel my fingers in my glove."

I usually played first base anyway, not the outfield. I could catch okay, but my throwing arm wasn't very strong. If by some fluke I would have to field the ball, I'd have to toss it over to Randy, the center fielder, and my co-worker, to throw into the infield to make the play. Don, being the best player on the team, was ensconced at short stop. Like I say, I usually played first base, and he didn't hesitate to drill the ball to me, his wife, at first base. But today, we were by some miracle in a final for the championships of our Great-West Life Softball league. Only the 'D' mixed division, but hey, a final! So, of course we'd stacked the positions for this important game and put a guy at first base. It was our third outing of the day, late September in Winnipeg, and it was not a warm day. Clouds scudded with the wind, the ever-present prairie wind. No rain, just the grey threatening kind of fall day that did not endear one to this city. Trees swayed past the fence, already bereft of leaves. At least the mosquitos that plagued the summer outfield were gone for the season. My fingers were numb as I hopped around to keep warm. As warm as possible in my green and black ball shirt over my long-sleeved undershirt. Randy smacked me on the back with his glove as he jogged over to position. Ooof!

The opposing team's pitcher tossed the softball to their own batter, and crack! A grounder, but right to Don covering second for the leftie hitter, and an easy throw to first. *One out! Play's to first, everyone!* But the next batter grounded past third, safe at first base. Tying run at the plate. *Look alive, people!* Then it happened, a right-handed hitter, but placing it high and short, to me, at right field! He probably aimed it like that. *Oh God, I lost it in the clouds, no, I've got it, I've got it!* Two away. Runner still stuck at first on the fly-out.

Somehow, we made another out. And then it was over. We won the 'D' Final! *I'm frozen, let's get to the banquet in the community hall right away!* Our game was the last one to finish, so we're the last team to show up.

The steamy heavenly warmth inside the hall smells like nirvana. We scramble to our team's reserved table and down the glasses of water set out there. It's a rush and hustle in the noisy hall, clinks of glasses, laughing and beer bottles everywhere. The lineup to the buffet seems long but moves at a good pace, and there it all is—a homemade Manitoba-Ukrainian feast of dishes wafting spicy smells in their crockpots and large oven pans. Perogies drenched in butter and bacon. Sausages all shapes and colours and sizes, buns and salads. Hot potato dishes simmering in pans of peppered cream. I fill my plate and am salivating as I sneak first bites of pickled beets and cheese squares.

We eat until interrupted by the announcer at the front of the hall: Attention, time to pass out the awards. And amid jokes and laughter and good friends and food, we accept our ribbons and medals emblazoned with "Great-West Life Softball Champions, 'D' Division 1985."

Every time I look at it, I feel the warmth and can taste the paprika in the meatballs.

This story reminds me that two factors can make a food or meal memorable: a celebration, plus true, hard-earned hunger, especially if earned outside in the fresh open sky. Here's another sports-inspired eating story. No championship, just the celebration of a happy life being lived.

"Mmm... potato dust!"

It's a cookie-cutter hot summer day, brilliant blue sky and not a hint of cloud, and Patti and I are young teenagers, tanned and scrawny and sitting in the shade on the grass in front of the Rec Centre on our home radar station, a military outpost set in prairie fields miles outside of Yorkton, Saskatchewan. Our long straight hair, Patti's bleached even blonder from the swimming pool, mine brown, has already dried in tangled strings after an afternoon spent in the outdoor pool at the back of the recreation complex. The towels we sit on are still damp. Why bother changing out of our two-piece suits for the walk home when we'll dry easily in the sun, still high before suppertime? Our after-swim treat? Potato chips of course, and after licking the first few from each of our bags, we've crushed the remainder into a pourable powder to drain directly into our mouths. Salt and vinegar, held together by the starchy crunch, mixed with saliva to pasty tasty lumpiness, to be savoured and enjoyed slowly. Or barbeque, that leave our licked fingers bright red with food dye. Like me, Patti can delay gratification. It becomes a reverse race to see whose chips can last the longest. A ten-cent bag can't last forever, however. Sighing with regret at their completion, we stand up and walk inside the building to toss the folded empty plastic Old

Dutch packages in the garbage can and to drink water from the fountain in the hallway outside the gymnasium. Time to go home for supper. We'll be back tomorrow. Nothing like splashing for hours, swimming, playing, fighting, flirting, working up an appetite to fuel a hunger so pure and real that salt and vinegar chips are the most delicious food on earth. Summers when you're thirteen are endless, and not in a bad way.

Nowadays, five decades away from the joy of those dreamy afternoons, my husband and I will go swimming once or twice a week. We'll drive. Horseplay and bobbing aren't appropriate at seniors lane swim times. We'll do our half hour of laps in an orderly direction. Then we'll shower and change into dry clothes and drive to a Vietnamese restaurant for a healthy lunch of Pho soup or a noodle dish for me. But if I close my eyes and inhale the fish sauce, the vinegar transports me back; I'm thirteen again, enjoying those satisfying potato chips on a hot summer day with Patti.

Restaurants

I eat in restaurants more now than when I was younger. I think this is true for many people. I wonder why?

I'll do a history lesson here. I'll call it "Restaurants: Their Role in One Middle Class Canadian's Life from the 1960s to Today." No empirical evidence to present, no data to compile, no definition of "middle class" to offer, although I always assumed that my family life was middle class. We never starved, nor did we ever go on family vacations by airplane to Disneyland. This essay is one author's observations, as deduced by anecdotal personal experience only.

1960s

In the 1960s, a restaurant to me as a child living on military bases in either Calgary, Germany, or Goose Bay meant either:

1. a German *gasthof* (an inn with a pub and restaurant on the main floor; technically translates as "guesthouse")

2. the Sergeant's Mess

All other references to restaurants meant little to me, other than as a place my parents might go to for their anniversary or other such special occasions for grownups. They were certainly not a place for children. We didn't have McDonalds anywhere I lived in the 1960s, or Dairy Queen, or even a small-town bar and grill. My experience with the *gasthofs* in Germany was as a place to have supper after a family Sunday drive that might have included a visit to a castle, like the one at nearby Altena. My parents would caution us to behave out in public, but I remember most *gasthofs* as convivial, full of other families with children at tables while parents drank large, long glass boots of fizzy golden beer, or tall dark bottles with rubber stoppers held by metal brackets that flipped open. I guess we only went at family mealtimes, because my husband, who also lived in Germany with his own family as a teenager, remembers *gasthofs* as simply beer drinking establishments, where the younger teens were only allowed to stay until about 9:00 p.m., at which time they were shooed out. To stumble home and try to avoid their severely judgmental Canadian parents after having blown their 14-year-old allowances for the week on German "pop." But that's a teenage story.

My own prepubescent experience of *gasthofs* were of the food. Meals were always ordered for us children by our parents, or come to think of it, maybe we ate whatever the *gasthof* had on special that day. For sure it included fat, greasy sausages that arrived sizzling alongside mashed potatoes, or better yet, with thick-cut French fries. And the mayonnaise! This is where I learned to eat French fries. The mayonnaise was thicker and more yellow than any I ate at home or ever since back in Canada. I don't remember much about vegetables. Maybe a wilted salad came served in a big bowl on the table for sharing, family-style? More likely some kind of sauerkraut, and most likely it was purple. There was a big wicker basket lined in white linen of *brochens*, buns hot and crispy outside and soft and white inside. I do remember the schnitzels, which to this day I will get a craving for and order the wiener version of it. Come to think of it, I probably only ate the wiener schnitzel at the Mess; it would have been too large a cut of meat and therefore too expensive for our family of six to order for us all each at the *gasthof*. I'm sure my parents had it, though.

The Mess. My dad was a sergeant, so if we went to a mess, it was the Sergeant's Mess, always the best mess on an army base. The Junior Ranks mess was for the wild young army guys, a drinking place for those hooligans to hang out at. And the Officer's Mess was snobby. The best mess was always the Sergeant's. Most sergeants were established family men, and I can't tell you when or where I first had a restaurant meal at the mess because they were pretty similar on every military base we ever lived. Nice long tables with white tablecloths and thick heavy white plates. Multiple glass types: for Father's beer, our water, and smaller ones for juice or milk. Very heavy cutlery, including sharp knives, which my brothers would use for swordplay, although to be fair, we were all quite well-behaved at the mess. It had been a rare treat we dressed up for. There was a variety of cakes and pies to anticipate for dessert. I don't think we had table service often—maybe for a Christmas or Thanksgiving or other such special meal at the mess. We'd usually walk to the back of the room toward the kitchen, which rang with soft clinking and clanking, to get served by the mess staff. You didn't pick anything out yourself, (except the dessert after the meal); you accepted what was dished out. A slab of some kind of meat like pink, salty ham steak, or chicken coated in some crumbly coating. Always potatoes, mashed or baked or roasted. I loved the roasted potatoes from the mess, so greasy and burnt just right. They were served with huge chunks of roast. I finally understood that meat did come from haunches of large animals like cows, because the roasts sitting on wood planks behind the huge stainless-steel serving counter were recognizable as such. I hadn't been raised on a farm, like my parents, so was fascinated to see such large hunks of cooked meat, bones showing. My brothers and I called roast beef, "roast beast." The vegetables served were never anything to recall, though, being plain beans or carrots. Lots of gravy and white buns called dinner rolls. I didn't eat the buns, needing to save room for cake multi-layered with thick seams of icing. Or for the lemon meringue pie, almost as good as what my mother made.

1970s

I moved into my teen years in the early 1970s. Petawawa, Ontario was about ten miles away from a big civilian town of Pembroke. A quick note about miles versus kilometers: I was part of the generation that started life with imperial units, like miles, and then moved to the metric system somewhere along the way. It's still confusing to me. I lived with kilometers in Germany, then miles back in Canada until whenever we changed? Sometime in my teens, I think.

Life was quite different for a growing family on a huge army base like Petawawa, Ontario compared to our little station life in Yorkton, Saskatchewan, where again, the only restaurant I remember had still been the sergeant's mess. Mom started working outside the home. My brothers and I made our own breakfasts and lunches. I became responsible for peeling potatoes for almost every weekday night. But weekends might now include a family dinner out to a restaurant, especially to a Chinese food restaurant, a drive into Pembroke. Long menus with unpronounceable items (so pick by the number), where everyone (including my then-boyfriend, future-husband Don) would pick out a dish to be shared family-style, placed steaming on the round turntable in the center of the large table. Mom would order the type of rice, and of course always an egg roll and wonton soup for all.

Soon Don and I would go out for our own couples' dinners. I had an income from lifeguarding. We'd go to Dixie Lee, like a KFC, where I would order the scallops meal served with fries and coleslaw. Or the local pizza parlour: mushroom, pepperoni, and green olives was our combo. Pembroke got a McDonald's the last year I lived in Petawawa because I remember Mom and I driving into town for lunch there the fall of 1976, just before I got married. No, I can't remember what we ate, but since McDonald's is McDonald's, well, you can guess.

The 1970s ended much differently from how they started. I was married and Don was a private in the military. We'd moved to Edmonton. Although I also continued to work as a lifeguard, I was a full-time student paying my own way at the University of Alberta. We were living the poorest years of our lives; at the lowest income level we'd ever have. It was not uncommon to scrounge dimes and quarters from pockets and piggy banks to buy a can of soup near the end of the pay period. We didn't have a credit card, which was a good thing, as I'm sure we'd have been in a bad debt way. I look back on those years not with any playful reminiscence, but with respect, as years for lessons in frugality. Dinners out? Not often. But, yes, on our wedding anniversary, for example, to places like The Keg, for the full steak-dinner experience, a whole night out's worth of entertainment.

1980s: Girls Just Want to Have Fun

Don and I were finally starting what would become better-paying careers, not yet as middle-class as we would become, but definitely able to afford eating out more often and for no other reason than enjoyment. I think I realized we were becoming richer in this story:

Edmonton. Don, a corporal in the air force, had just been accepted to become an officer and needed to take his basic officer training in Chilliwack, British Columbia. I was still a university student, but had progressed to a union-waged lifeguard job in the city, off the base, and made much better money. We'd just bought a brand-new car, a 1980 black two-door Datsun 200SX. Don would be on military training in Chilliwack, but it so happened that my own father had retired from the military himself in Chilliwack and my parents both still worked and lived there. I would visit and stay with them for a whole month. But first, road trip, which included a night's stopover somewhere in the Rockies, I can't even remember what town. I checked into a motel with a restaurant attached. And went over for supper.

It was a bright, cozy, sparsely populated dining room, still early enough that it wasn't too busy. The waitress was polite and matronly. I had to show ID to order a cocktail, and after some chitchat about why I was travelling alone, she warmed up; I think she decided I needed some mothering.

"What'll you have, dear?" she asked. When I said I didn't know and asked what she would suggest, she replied that I needn't worry, she'd get something nice for me. The chef had a daily special.

Well, nice? It was fantastic. First, bread and butter, hot and homemade. Then a small salad, and not iceberg lettuce as was the norm for these times. A hot gravied cutlet of something, pork tenderloin, I think, with mashed potatoes and green beans, the long string kind. I was getting full, but dessert was included and wouldn't disappoint. Strawberry shortcake with real whipped cream. I'd been used to Dream Whip and couldn't believe whipped cream could be this good. I had a tea with Grand Marnier too.

A little whoozy from the full meal and alcohol, the waitress told me not to worry; they'd add the price to the hotel bill. She walked me outside to watch that I made it back to my room safely. Of course, the next morning I had a shock—the meal had cost more than the motel room! But it did open my eyes about how good food at a restaurant could be. And that I might now be able to afford it.

There was no looking back, the 1980s would be eating-in-restaurants years.

Of course, all meals weren't three or four courses and expensive. Don and I would go out for supper more often for other important reasons, like laziness. Or at least a lack of interest in cooking when there was so much excitement to live outside the home. No children yet, no responsibilities other than to ourselves. Lots of work: college then full-time work, nine-to-five. Nights of sports activities: curling and softball and hockey. Going to the gym. Lots of different groups of friends. These were the pub years, Chinese food, pizza, burgers, and fries; most meals came with fries. But there still were the special restaurant times for anniversaries or when relatives came to visit. Outings for food had two purposes—the older tradition of going to the nicest restaurant our current situation could afford for special occasions, and a newer reason, which was to go out with friends for a fun, casual, social time.

For example, wedding anniversaries in the 1980s: Kingston, Ontario. Fancy white table-cloth seafood restaurant, where as the lady, I was handed a menu with no prices. Alaska King Crab then, please. I never did find out what Don had to pay. Another one in Kingston: a star-rated hotel (now a chain that Don and I have member cards with), where again, seafood seemed my exotic meal of choice, and I had arctic char. Some people claim arctic char is just salmon from up north, but they must have never tasted what I did that anniversary. I've never had better: flaky, tasty, oily with the skin on. Served with little roasted fingerling potatoes and fancy vegetables arranged into designs. Unfortunately, that magical anniversary night out was also a school night, an exam-eve in fact for an important college class. I didn't fail the test the next day, but I muddled through it and attracted teacher attention and extra assignments with my low mark. I still don't regret that fish, though.

1990s

We started the 1990s in Cold Lake, Alberta, with two small boys and me unemployed for a stint. Luckily, it was cheap enough to live in military PMQs, and there weren't many restaurants to blow money on. We did eat at the Officers Mess more often. They had a wild game night that I recall as delightful: venison stew, duck confit, smoked roast of bear. Actually, the bear was terrible, a dark gamey taste that I can recall but have never again encountered. I'm told that's because it was smoked, but sorry, that's the only way I've ever had it, and I'm not missing it.

Soon Don would be posted back to the civilization of the city, to Ottawa, where we found ourselves living on the Québec side of the river. With children and careers to nurture, restaurants became as much a part of our family eating routine as eating at home, but a new type of eating out was the reason: convenience. McDonald's, sure, Tim Hortons, absolutely, but not as much as local family diners or chains for chicken dinners or spaghetti. Or pizza places with salad bars; any place we could afford. Money was still tight with all the middle-class consumerism to keep up with: cars, mortgage, kids' activities. And hockey. Kid's hockey, the major expense of my life, was beginning.

Finally, in these years a major breakthrough in restaurant eating occurred: smoke-free areas, which didn't last too long until all restaurants where I lived were 100% smoke-free. It's hard to remember now how awful it used to be to go out to dinner and have the couple sitting next to you lean over and ask, "Do you mind if I smoke?" No matter that you did mind, you always politely replied, "Please, go ahead," while they lit up. What were we thinking? But that was the way it was. I've mentioned Tim Hortons, but I never went into a donut shop on my own volition until well into the 1990s, when even the donut shops finally became smoke-free. Before that, I remember boxes of donuts brought to the office that wafted the putrid smell of cigarette smoke when the lids to the dozens were lifted. "Michele, don't you like donuts?" I would be asked. Maybe, how would I know, because the only ones available had been those tobacco-flavoured ones.

Of course, Don and I still tried to keep up our special restaurant anniversary tradition, but it was strained in these busy years. Sometimes it was just a lunch meeting at the pub near my office. We did take the day off for our twenty-fifth, and after a hike in the nearby Gatineau hills on that bright, unseasonably warm October day, we dropped in for a late lunch at a high-end French cuisine restaurant downtown Hull. We had a romantic seat in a window alcove, warm afternoon sunshine streaming in.

Appetizers of frog legs. Toasting ourselves with a bottle of white wine, kept cool in the iced aluminum vase and poured wrapped in the white napkin, on which we splurged, because unfortunately we couldn't finish it. We had to be back by school pickup time to take kids to hockey practices.

Yes, the 1990s were speeding by, and by the 2000s, things wouldn't be much slower.

2000s

About all I can remember about the 2000s is being a hockey parent. Buffets were becoming popular, especially after games with other hockey families, where the boys could gorge and parents could drink.

2010s

By now, the boys were in college, out of town in separate directions. Don and I would visit one or the other on weekends and of course, take our son of the moment out for a nice Saturday night supper, usually pub style, and usually after his hockey game. Then out again for a big breakfast on Sunday morning before we left for home. Breakfast was becoming a trendy meal out, but I never loved it. The meals were too large. My sons would happily finish my eggs and home fries, or at least take the leftovers back to their dorm room to eat after they got up from their second sleep later that Sunday afternoon.

At home, Don and I were adjusting to cooking for two, and honestly, restaurant meals were becoming tiresome. Or maybe my life was becoming tiresome. Work all week and travel most weekends. Hotels and restaurants added to the grind.

Beyond

Of course, boys grow up, get jobs and wives and lives of their own. Don and I retired. Restaurants have regained their place in our lives; we've come back to enjoying them. The variety available in a city region like Ottawa-Gatineau is endless. Now, pub food is for friends again, after a curling or bowling outing, or for a downtown lunch and museum trip. Fancy restaurants are for food that I cannot or will not make myself. I've found a steak place that means I'll never cook one at home ever again—how do they get it so tender? My early love of Chinese food has morphed into specific Asian fare, with Thai and Vietnamese being favourites. Better yet, the Asian fusion—such an excellent idea that is: mixing, borrowing, blending food cultures for a new whole better enjoyment.

Some people think that restaurant eating will wane in the future, as if we'll have drones delivering our food directly from robot-chefs. My own condo building already sees multiple daily deliveries of those boxes of pre-measured ingredients that you can cook up yourself. Yes, I agree, it can be easier than ever to eat well at home.

But I doubt that the reasons we go out for dinner will completely disappear: to eat different food, in different settings, with other people. To celebrate, to belong. I think it's human nature to congregate for food consumption, even if that congregation is of strangers in a restaurant. There's something primal and cozy about that. I don't imagine giving it up at all.

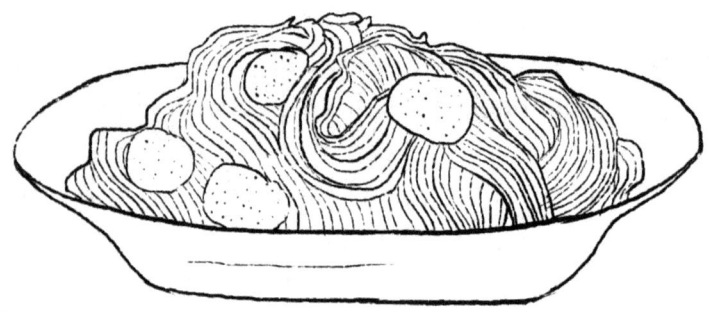

Diet Chapter and Lessons from Women

You can't write stories about food without mentioning *that* 'D' word. I know the noun diet can simply mean the types and amounts of food one eats. But we more commonly refer to it as a plan that restricts or limits what we eat, usually in order to lose weight. We'll also use the word as a verb, as in, "I'm dieting to shed a few pounds."

I've had my experiences with diets. How could I not, being a woman of Western society in her sixth decade? I'd have to have lived in a cave where I'd never experienced societal pressures and advice. And most of my life was before the internet! These days, it seems like there is even more pressure and confusing information than when I had to deal with thin cover models on magazines that spouted nonsense articles like, "Flat Tummy in One Hour!" These would be the same magazines, by the way, to offer a triple-layer cream cheesecake recipe.

"Oh, Michele, you're lucky, you're naturally skinny."

As if being called skinny was a compliment. I happen to think that any size is fine if you're healthy and happy. So, it always annoyed me, this comment. How often have I heard it, trivializing my own struggles at times with uncomfortable creeping weight gain? I know that men also struggle with weight control, but in my experience, it's a topic that women often share with each other. Personally, I have maintained a relatively steady weight throughout my life, despite some ups and downs that I wasn't happy with. I credit such maintenance to many factors, and although some are not in my control (I didn't pick my parents), many of them are. I've learned many lessons from people, especially from the women in my life, to figure out these factors. The first and foremost being the family food practices of my childhood.

I don't know if I'm lucky, but I did grow up in a family that didn't have large body types, so genetics must have contributed something. My father, in his eighties now, is skinnier than when he was younger, as was his mother, my grandmother, in her elderly years. And none of his four kids, myself included, became over-comfortable-weight into middle age. We were also an active family where sports were a natural part of the day. My father was a military physical training instructor, after all. I played ball, walked everywhere, swam. We all had bikes. We also were financially challenged enough and my mother clever enough, that meal portion sizes were limited to reasonable amounts. And dessert?

Only on birthdays, Christmas, Thanksgiving, and Easter. Which, in a family of six, meant about once a month. Maybe more in the summer when my father might get the banana split craving after supper. We'd all pile into the car, dog included, to head on a dessert road trip to the nearest ice cream parlour, like Dairy Queen (which was quite far away sometimes, as in Yorkton). But sweets weren't an everyday occurrence.

All suppers at home had been eaten family-style around a dining room table. Except for occasional invites in or out—of four kids, there might always be one missing or bringing a friend—all breakfasts and suppers were at home, and supper was always all six of us together. It's hard to imagine this kind of routine today. It certainly didn't work out like that for my own family, raising two boys in sports while both of us parents worked fulltime.

I didn't realize how different family eating styles could be until I was fifteen and invited over to my first supper out at my then-boyfriend Don's house. My future father-in-law was a big man, and both he and my future mother-in-law grew up during the depression. Both valued food as a source of love and most of all—security. My 90-something mother-in-law today still has fully stocked cupboards and a freezer full of her baking and extra meals, packaged and ready for the apocalypse, despite which, I've pointed out, would probably include power outages. Back to that first meal of spaghetti at her house:

"Wow, who else is coming over for dinner?" I asked.

There was the largest pot I'd ever seen on the stove; it covered three burners. Wait, I had seen such pots. In the army mess. As military kids, we'd all had meals, cafeteria-style, where chili or something creamy like it would be ladled onto our toast or bread by a white-hatted private from such-a-sized pot. This one now was bubbling with water for the spaghetti to be cooked in.

"No one else is coming over but you, dear. Why do you ask?"

Flummoxed, really, I only asked if I could help. Maybe set the table. Really, what else could I say? I wondered how much spaghetti was going to be cooked. If shock was what I expected, I was not to be disappointed with the result. As at the mess, we brought our plates to the kitchen to be ladled by Mom, the cook.

I had to stop her, "Uh, that's enough, thank you." I'd never seen spaghetti piled, only spread, on the plate. "And one scoop of sauce is plenty, wow, thank you," I stammered.

Wow is right.

"Oh, eat up; you're not on a diet, are you? I hope not, you're skinny enough! What do you weigh, dear? What's your waist measurement? Mine was twenty-two inches in my wedding dress. I still weigh under 130, and I've had three children."

What? We didn't own a scale at home. But I

was quick later to try theirs in the bathroom—120 pounds. I felt like an ox.

As Dad, Don, and his two brothers piled and piled their spaghetti, I could only watch, mesmerized. I did notice Mom took less than she'd given me. And she didn't even finish it. I'd never seen food left on plates at home. These boys didn't leave any, either. And then came dessert, which to be fair, I assumed was because it was a special supper, with me, the girlfriend, invited over. Brownies, still warm from the oven, their heavy, sweet aroma drifting from the kitchen, and vanilla ice cream, scooped direct from the carton right at the table. Delicious. Still, not a typical supper for me.

I did remember the lesson of my mother-in-law, though. She needed to feed big men with active lives, not unlike my grandmother, now that I recall, yet she maintained control over her own portions. This was valuable information that would return to me as a theme forever after. Eating in restaurants? You don't have to eat all the fries they bring, but you can still order the burger with the fries. At a party? Just eat a smaller piece of the cake, not the huge portion you will be handed. I went one better on this one, especially in the years at office jobs where cake was brought in for everyone's' birthdays: I only ate the icing. Yes, people stared. At first, I was embarrassed and slipped the cake leftovers in the garbage at my own desk, but soon, it was "a thing Michele did," and actually, I later found a partner to eat the cake part while I ate his icing part. Enjoy what you want, eat your favourite part, but don't eat what you don't need because of peer pressure, especially if it's cake!

So, family upbringing in my case was a big contributor to a lifetime of moderately successful weight control while enjoying food. I would meet other women and learn about dieting for weight control from them. Here are more of those stories and what they taught me.

The Doctor

Like many people at the age of twenty-two, I considered myself in peak condition. I swam laps almost daily, and worked out with weights in the gym to keep my strength up for constant lifeguarding exams. I was a university student and walked a lot around the campus. I was married, but we only had one car and my husband worked shift work back then, so I had to walk to the base pool to work, regardless of weather, which really mattered in climates like Edmonton, Alberta. I was fit and healthy. So why, at a regular yearly checkup, did the doctor say to me in her office after the exam, "You're overweight. Do you eat a lot of pasta? Kraft Dinner? Like most young people?"

Confused, rattled, I blurted that yes, of course I ate Kraft Dinner. Who didn't? *But wait—*

"Why do you say I'm overweight? I weighed 122 on your scale! I'm almost five foot four. That's not overweight!"

"Yes, it's two pounds overweight. You young

people...you will gain a pound a year, and by age forty, you'll be obese at one hundred and forty pounds. Stop the macaroni. More salads. Other than that, all looks good. Watch your weight. See you in a year."

I was flabbergasted. Nobody in my whole life had ever, ever called me overweight. I soon got a little angry. As I've mentioned, my father was an army physical trainer. I'd learned sports science and fitness knowledge at his knee my whole life. I knew that muscle weighed more than fat and that I was muscular for my size. I wasn't overweight, nor was I on track to become obese at age forty. And who thinks 140 pounds is obese anyway—who did this doctor think she was?

Actually, I have since learned that most general practitioners were not, nor are they yet, experts on weight management. I am not advocating for ignoring doctor advice. This episode is relayed for two reasons:

Doctors are human. They advise with your best interest at heart. But they often just apply statistical knowledge to individual cases. This is fair—they can't personally know each and every patient. Today I accept that doctor's opinion as following her best attempt at helping me with my health.

I was determined to prove that doctor wrong. The rebel in me would not gain a pound a year to become "obese" by age forty. And, although I couldn't tell you exactly how, my stubbornness to be right prevailed and I maintained a weight that works for me. My weight at age 40 hadn't remained at 122 pounds, but it certainly wasn't close to being an "obese" 140. So, in retrospect, thanks, Doc!

Here are more stories of some diets I've never followed. Or maybe followed some, for a while. But not really.

The Diet Queens

I learned one diet lesson from a friend who I met in college in Kingston after university in Edmonton (it's that military moving story again). She was tall, fit, buxom, athletic. An Amazon. I admired her and her figure, clearly opposite to my own short, non-buxom one. But like her beautiful, naturally wavy hair, which she wished was straight like mine (I wanted curly and had many perms to prove it), she wished she was slimmer. So, every once in a while at the college pub, she'd declare, "No beer for me. I'm on my diet. Just water." They were always "her" diets. How long this time? They were real diets, following a printed plan, and lasted a specific length of time. There were one-week diets, weekday diets, month-long diets, all with names I can't recall. I never made fun of the grapefruit-only or no-carbs or only-carbs, nor of any of the other restrictive eating regimes. At first I was uncomfortable eating and drinking in front of Joan while she was on her diet of the day, but that was my own problem. Joan never complained or looked longingly at my hamburger. She was tough; she strictly adhered. And soon, she would lose weight. I found it impressive that she could lose weight with sheer willpower.

But invariably, after the diet, Joan would return to her pre-diet weight. I don't think she ate more than anybody, and we all drank too much in college. She was and still is an active athlete: bikes, plays ball, hikes. And no one knows nutrition better than her. Over the years she studied and followed more diets than anyone I ever knew. But she's still not as slim today as she always wanted to be.

The lesson? Everyone's different. Some of us are slim and some of us are not. Be healthy, be yourself. It's my favourite diet lesson of all.

The Party Girl Diet

The worst diet advice I ever got also came in my younger years. I called it the "Party Girl Diet." Simply, it was, you drank alcohol until you didn't feel like eating food. This was not to say that anyone ever planned to lose weight by solely drinking alcohol. This was merely observation of fact. One drink made one hungry. So you'd have another gin and lemonade. Hmmm...still hungry? Maybe, so have another. Then the burgers were ready or the salads placed on the table. But darn, another drink sounds better, so, by magic, after only drinking, you didn't eat your supper! Concerned about the calories from the three or four cocktails? Sugar-laden though they were, don't fret; they will be thrown up by midnight! Voilà. I personally never followed this routine, but am relaying it "for a friend."

Another terrible idea: smoke cigarettes. I knew many a young woman who smoked to curb their appetite. Me? Never. "Cancer-sticks" might make one skinny, but was it worth it? This is rhetorical.

I'm sure there are other terrible diet ideas, like the amphetamines that were actually prescribed as diet pills in the 1960s, but I never personally knew anyone who dieted with them. (That I knew of; how would I know? It wouldn't have been discussed.) I did babysit for one young couple in the early 1970s who left a box of what looked and tasted like caramels on their kitchen counter. It was labelled as a diet aid; eat one before meals to curb one's appetite. As I said, they looked like caramels, and yes, I snuck one or two while babysitting. They didn't seem to curb my teenage appetite. Oh, the name of the product stuck with me, though; they were called Ayds. Obviously, this product never made it into the 1980s.

The Women of Steel Diets

"I only eat every second day." So declared Rhoda.

Rhoda was in the military, something I was still getting used to; my life had been fairly sheltered growing up a military kid in PMQs. At this point, I was a young Air Force wife living at CFB Edmonton in the late 1970s. Rhoda, a few other hockey wives, and I were chatting in the lobby at the rink before game time, where, as is common when young women who don't know each other are forced into conversation, the discussion had turned to food and dieting.

"What do you mean, you only eat every second day? You mean you *don't* eat anything every other day?" someone asked.

Rhoda was thin and athletic. It seemed unbelievable to me that someone wouldn't eat for a whole day.

"It's called fasting. It's good for you. No, I don't get hungry, well, yes, I guess I feel hunger, but I like it. And I eat whatever I want the next day. It's no big deal."

I don't remember much else about Rhoda, but after that admission, I did think she was peculiar. Either she was lying—I'd never heard of people fasting on purpose—or she was strange in some other way. Of course, over the years, I came to understand that fasting is a choice many people make, and there is even recent research that it is good for you. (This is not an endorsement. I myself have never made it a full 24 hours, so can't speak from any experience.) The lesson here was: don't judge. We all have our own relationships with food. I judged then. But I learned I shouldn't have.

The last I heard of Rhoda, she was happy and married to the goalie she'd been dating back then and had two kids.

But I continued to encounter Rhoda-types throughout my life.

I've always been a gym goer, and have had my share of body compliments and comments over the years. "What are you training for?" I'd be asked from time to time. Or, "What exercises do you do for your legs? You have great calves." At first I didn't understand such questions. I'd been more used to the sexist questions of my youth, such as, "Aren't you worried you'll get muscles doing the bench press?" Yes, I was really asked that once. But more women were coming to the weight rooms now, and bodybuilding was in vogue. It was the early 1980s.

At the gym, women bodybuilders would spend as much time discussing their training diets as they did lifting weights. Powdered protein drinks were all the rage; blenders were *de rigeur* after the *Rocky* movies showed boxers downing drinks made with raw eggs. Whacky diets consisted of no carbs one week, no protein the next, and never any fat, nor even water the last days before competitions. This would be to get body fat down to ridiculous levels, levels low enough to show muscle strands. Low enough to pose all oiled up and fake-bronzed, but not low enough to faint on-stage. Maybe to faint just after the show, though, that would be alright. I know those body-builder ladies quickly downed brownies and wine and bread right after their on-stage performance and would often gain pounds of weight and fat back within weeks, even days afterwards. It seemed extreme me, and I never did any of that, despite working out on weights for years in gyms with people who did.

And as I age, the body comments don't stop, they're just a little different. "Wow, for someone who exercises so much, why is your pot so big?" Sigh, yes, this again was a real comment in the change room after swimming once. I wish I hadn't been upset by the remark then, because it's actually quite funny. Two kids and six decades leave their mark. The final lesson: do the best you can with what you've got.

My Favourite Evil Food

All this to say, I've never really dieted. I live with a diet, of course, one of sensible whole, real foods. Milk. Oatmeal. Bread. Butchered meats bought in plastic-wrap (becoming more paper-wrapped nowadays, again, like when I was a kid), not in boxes pre-salted or injected with cheese.

Vegetables that need to be cleaned and chopped, or come frozen in whole, unaltered state, not coated in creamy sauces.

This is not to say I never splurge. I have my problem foods and habits to keep watch on. And I know there are no "evil" foods—everything in moderation. This is my story of what either I can't eat due to side effects, or, truth be told, what I will occasionally eat despite the side effects.

Number 1 on the list: Potato chips. If I had to pick something for my last meal while awaiting execution on death row (I wonder what I did?), it would be sour cream and onion potato chips.

I'm 19. I live in Brantford, Ontario, and I work as a lifeguard full-time for the summer while my husband is doing his basic training in Cornwallis, Nova Scotia. I'm as fit and tan as I ever will be in my life. I just got my driver's license a few weeks earlier, in Renfrew, Ontario while on a June visit to my parents in Petawawa, before my father's military posting to Chilliwack, British Columbia. I could drive to work here in Brantford, but it's a reasonable bike ride, so that's what I do. I do eat a good breakfast of cereal, toast, and juice every day, and take a sandwich for my lunch. I only work day shifts—the evening shifts are for the high school kid lifeguards. I'm the experienced, older, married woman. By the time my shift ends at 5:00 p.m., and I ride my bike home to our apartment in the upstairs of a pre-World War II brick house, I'm both exhausted and ravenous. A big glass of water and a 220-gram bag of Hostess Sour Cream and Onion potato chips awaits, and that's exactly what I eat four nights out of five that summer of 1977. Lactose gas attacks and calorie-counting were in my future. Close your eyes and enjoy them again with me (or be grossed out, I've been told): the first coated chip, heavily salted and powdered, lick it first. Tangy, oniony, salty, creamy. Roll the paste it makes around in your mouth. Breathe in the dust. Crunch it or let it sog up by licking both sides...your preference. Repeat. Repeat until the crumbs at the bottom of the bag are poured into your hand and licked up. Now re-lick your delicious fingers. Sigh.

Okay, wake up. This is not a potato chip endorsement article. I ate the salty delights far too often for my hypertensive genetics to handle. The mornings after the night before I would often be puffy, retaining water from the salt, thirsty for more water, then needing pee breaks once an hour for the first half of the day. Because I drank grapefruit juice at breakfast in these times, the potassium helped to balance the sodium and facilitate all the peeing. I knew it couldn't go on, and it didn't, but...ahh... those sure were the days.

Today? Sometimes a bowl (not a whole family-sized bag) of low-sodium chips, mixed in with organic blue potato chips, which can be found at health food stores for only about three times the cost of regular chips. And sometimes I even throw in a few flavoured chips in the bowl, like All-Dressed. Rarely anything with milk solids listed on the ingredients though. But sometimes. And chips are definitely planned to be included for any last meal I'm offered on my deathbed.

Other evil foods to list? I admit not many. Wine. Potato chips. Isn't that enough?

If I had to condense one lifetime of diet advice, again, it would only be one word: moderation. I eat in moderation. Almost anything I want, with the few restrictions I've already mentioned: only lactose-free dairy. Other self-imposed limits are the result of trial and error. I'm careful to restrict the salt in Asian food. I don't drink rum and coke, which seems to upset my stomach, but I do enjoy wine and sometimes a gin and tonic.

Life and food—the lessons are never-ending.

Lessons from Kids and Dogs

We all live in our own universe, one that's comprised of a mixture of choices and life's dice rolls. No one can experience or live in all possible universes. Not everyone has children, nor wants them, not everyone will have daughters, even if they wanted them. My life included giving birth to two boys. Same for pets: I loved them as a child, but never had one as an adult. My particular universe led to lessons in many of life's categories, and of course, in the category of food.

D'Arcy and the Cookies and Pie

"The first one's made of glass; the second one's made of rubber." So quoted my mother to me in her careful grandmotherly-critique voice. You know it, right?

"In my day, kids were given aspirin if they were hyper!"

As new parents, of course we couldn't understand

how our parents' generation managed to raise any of us at all, with nonsense such as that for advice.

"The baby's hungry, put a little cereal in his formula bottle."

Horrors! "Bad enough" he's on formula, not breast milk. The least we could do was follow the doctor's strict orders of not giving him cereal for the first three months.

"Do you want him to get allergies?" asked our doctor.

No. I'd suffered from eczema all my life and now realized where I might have got it from:

"Baby food?" my mother would query, "Just mush up your own meal."

Actually, I'm told that one's back as fine for my grandkids. Who can keep track with parenting rules over the generations anyway? My own mother wouldn't let her children (me) drink coffee, but my son told me Grandma let him drink it when he visited, as long as he "didn't tell Mom" (me).

I guess like all new parents, we could be accused of over-protecting D'Arcy, our first-born. Only healthy food. No sweets. Occasionally a sugared Mini-Wheat, which we called cookies. He seemed good with them, even preferring the frozen peas as a snack over the cookies. Unfortunately, other Grandma was a cookie-baker, and worse, the kind that doesn't eat much of her own cooking but wants everyone else to stuff themselves with it. Carrot cake, moist, rich with raisins and walnuts, extra icing, real, cream-cheese icing. But only a sliver for her; she was always watching her figure.

During the first visit with the two-year-old grandchild in Brantford after the long summer drive from Winnipeg, Grandma asks, "D'Arcy, do you want a cookie? I've baked special chocolate chip cookies just for you!"

She did, too.

"Oh yes! Pease Gamma, pease, I yike cookies." He did. What he thought were cookies, of course.

"Uck!" Then, "P-tooh," right back out on the plate.

"What's the matter, D'Arcy? Don't you like my cookies?"

Uh-oh.

"No! Tings in it!"

Yes, things. Chocolate chips. Grandma was shocked and tried not to be offended. We were so embarrassed.

At about the same time, my own Grandmother was still living, in Killarney, Manitoba. Being in Winnipeg, a three-hour drive away, we would visit when we could. D'Arcy was a favourite of Great-Grandma, as he could pack it away at three years old and of course GG, like many of her generation, liked to see a chubby boy with a big appetite.

"Better grocery bills than doctor bills," was her view.

I grew up with free health care. Doctor bills, like doctor home visits, were not relatable. But again, like stereotype Grandmas everywhere in those days, mine could bake. Her pies were the best: flaky, white crust (extra lard), and always fillings from her own backyard garden. Raspberries, plums, and especially apples—the extra-tart crab apple kind she loaded up with sugar for a unique sweet-sour deliciousness that cannot be bought in a store.

Getting ready to leave after one visit, I asked, "Grandma, when are you making another apple pie? I haven't had one for a while."

"Oh," she said, "I made extra last fall and froze them. Do you want to take one home?"

Of course! So, we put the frozen uncooked pie in a plastic bag and hugged our goodbyes. Curious, D'Arcy wondered what was in the plastic bag.

"It's Great-Grandma's famous apple pie. We'll bake it when we get home, okay? What do you think?"

"Oh yes, pie, I yike pie! I want pie!" Hmm...he'd never had pie, this I knew; I certainly had never baked one.

On the drive home, as usual, our busy little boy napped. Home by supper time, D'Arcy was a good kitchen helper, and he hadn't forgotten about the pie. We put it in the oven together and looked at it through the murky glass window in front. (I know now it was murky because one must clean it regularly to keep it clear. Who knew?)

"It's pie, pie! I want pie!"

"Supper first, it'll take at least an hour to cook up."

"Yay, supper!"

After supper, the pie still wasn't ready. "Let's clean up. We'll read a book and put our jammies on. We'll have pie later, for dessert."

"What's dessert?"

"It's a treat after supper. Let's get ready."

"Yay, treatie!"

We watched the pie golden up in the oven. I opened and checked it with a knife in through the top in the centre and tested how hot. It seemed ready, bubbling up. "Smell those apples, D'Arcy, how wonderful, right?"

"Apple? I want pie."

"The pie is made with apples. Watch out, I'm taking it out now. Doesn't it look good?"

"Where the apple, Mommy? I want apple."

"The apples are cooked in the pie. You'll see."

"No. I want apple. No pie. Apple. AAA Apple!"

He ran to his father, reaching to the counter with the apples in the bowl. Don laughed and handed him an apple.

"No," I insisted, setting the pie on the towel on the counter. "We're having pie! Apple pie! Put that apple back. Don, help me out!" And then I heard myself. Arguing with a three-year-old to stop eating an apple so I could force him to eat pie! I burst out laughing myself. We put D'Arcy to bed after he finished his apple. Then Don and I ate delicious apple pie and watched TV.

As you might have guessed, D'Arcy liked to eat. I needed to carry snacks everywhere for those toddler years, else risk ferocious tantrums. Here's a sample of what was in my purse:

D'Arcy's Toddler Snack

In plastic Ziploc bags, add portion sizes of the following mixes.

Tip: only one portion per bag, as child will want to grab the bag and eat entire contents.

- Cheerios (or handfuls of any dry cereal)
- Raisins
- Crackers
- Cracker sandwiches glued together with peanut butter
- Frozen peas (you might want to put these in their own bag to account for the melt factor)

Interestingly, on a recent visit to grown-up D'Arcy's house, his wife Jessica was packing for a work trip. What are those bulk-sized bags and jars and boxes of stuff on the counter, I wondered? Then D'Arcy walked in and started putting handfuls from each into single-serving sized Tupperware-style containers. Homemade toddler-style snack portions! Nuts, cereals, dried fruits. He asked if I wanted one since he was making some for Jess's road trip and her night-time hotel nibbles. Also for his own week's worth of office snacks. The funny part, while explaining this all to me, was that he thought he'd invented this snack idea himself. I smiled.

Sasha - The Rubber Child

To this day, D'Arcy doesn't eat much sugary food. I don't know how much one is influenced by early eating habits. Was his aversion to sweets because we restricted it, or was it an inherent trait? No worries, we had another son to experiment with.

If we over-thought teaching food lessons and restricting "bad" food for our first child, it was easier to slack off with child number two, Sasha, also known as The Rubber One, who was taking sugar whenever he could get it. With a four-year-old big brother who didn't like sweets, and parents not as vigilant (second child and all), it was inevitable that he would get his fill. In fact, this leads me to a very cautionary tale:

Don't take candy from strangers—or from your hockey coach.

We didn't think to add that second piece of advice. I would if I ever got to relive my mom years over again, which, thank goodness, won't ever happen, barring some time machine invention. Maybe I'll save it as advice for my grandchildren's parents, who of course won't listen to their careful grandmother's advice any more than I listened to mine. Ah, the cycle of life.

The tale. We were living by then in our forever hometown, what would become our children's hometown and our retirement location, of Aylmer (later amalgamated into greater Gatineau), Québec. Both boys had settled into their childhood lifestyles of local schools, other sports, and above all, hockey. Don and I were working and advancing in our careers as much as possible to support them in this expensive and time-consuming pursuit. D'Arcy by now was playing on the highest-level regional team at twelve-years-old, and his younger nine-year-old brother was still on the local Novice team. But this Novice team was exceptional that year. They were, in fact, and would remain, undefeated the whole season. This included wins in every tournament they entered. And they entered a lot; I can recall the numerous championship banners lining a wall in our own arena but still can't remember how many. More than a dozen, for sure. The head coach was the father of the best eight-year-old on the team, a team where I'm obliged to report that my son was the star captain.

I do remember the following incident took place at one of Sasha's tournaments in Pembroke, Ontario, near where Don and I had gone to high school on the army base in Petawawa. Where I'd been to many games as a teenager, first to watch my father referee, later when my boyfriend played there. So, it was a fun away weekend for us to reminisce and visit old high school haunts. Military kids love going back to places they've lived; it isn't always possible as Canada's military presence shrinks over the decades. But I digress. I can't remember where D'Arcy was that weekend. I'm sure he stayed with friends to play his own games at home, back in Gatineau.

These kind of tournament weekends were great fun for parents. We stayed in hotels. The kids were really under the wings of the coaches and did all activities, even eating meals, together, leaving parents to drink and party and nurse hangovers at the games. Sasha would sleep in our hotel room but was on a strict schedule to be wherever and do whatever the hockey coaches had arranged for them. As the captain, he had duties with the coaching staff. (Yes, I remember he was only nine years-old.) Parents were there only as drivers and to hand over money for food and activities.

The parent volunteer approached us hanging out in the lobby before one of the final games of the tournament.

"Your share for the pre-game preparation is five dollars," he said. We paid, no questions. As usual. You didn't question all the cash outflow; it was nonstop. Besides, parents who questioned too much found kids cut from the team the following year. We had already been through all that routine (in fact, would live through many more years of it) with our older son.

But another parent was resistant. "What's the pre-game prep? What's this money for?"

"Oh, no big deal, just something to pump the kids up before the game."

This was interesting. What were the coaches doing to the kids to "pump them up?"

So, after the game—we certainly had no opportunity to speak with our son before any game—we asked Sasha what were the coaches giving the kids before the game for "prep?"

He was dodgy at first. We did the whole parent talk about making sure all was above board in the dressing room. And then he said:

"Josh didn't want to eat his power pill, so the coach benched him the first period."

What?! Stay calm. "What 'power pill?'"

"You know, just pieces of chocolate bars before the game, to pump us up. We call them our power pills. I know it's just chocolate, though. I wouldn't take pills, Mom."

No, you wouldn't. Not at nine years-old. But now I understand why elite athletes, Olympic champions even, will take drugs from their coaches, then later swear they didn't know what they were taking was anything illicit. Sounds incredible, but it is clear how it happened.

They'd been groomed and trained as children. And parents like us had let it happen.

Luckily, a lesson we learned young enough for our own kids. We made as many parenting mistakes as I assume all parents do, even more, but this is one I am glad to have caught. There were times later I learned that players were "pumping up" with energy drinks, coffee mixed with Tylenol, even other stuff, but my own kids always told us and swore they didn't do anything themselves.

I still sweat thinking about it.

Cognac

Yes, named for the booze.

The phone rang one weekday evening when I was 24 years old and living in Kingston, Ontario. This was in 1982. I was married to my Air Force husband and going to college. The call was not a regular Sunday after 6:00 p.m. call, when long-distance rates were in effect, so when I heard my mother's voice on the line from British Columbia, I instantly thought something wrong. It was.

"Cognac died last night," she said.

Cognac, my family's dog since 1969, acquired as a roly-poly puppy at the northern air base of Goose Bay, Labrador, had arrived on the spring morning of my 11th birthday party sleepover. A golden-red coloured Lab look-a-like, but smaller and fatter. He looked like a little beer bottle, the old stubby kind, with legs. White-tipped paws that scampered after us four kids, truly another little brother in the family. He would come with us on the rest of my dad's military postings: from Labrador by airplane and by car at my mother's feet across the country to Saskatchewan; back east again to Petawawa, Ontario, where I would be the first one to leave home. Another long trip west to Chilliwack, British Columbia, to end his years there.

As a pup in Labrador, Cognac was, like the rest of us, allowed wide open freedom. He'd bark to be let out—one short yelp—and bark to be let back in. We had a chain outside, but it was rarely used. Besides, his bull neck allowed many escapes from the collar. We had a harness at first for him, but he chewed it to pieces, so a choke-chain collar it would be from then on. He became a self-appointed guard dog, no matter that he never grew higher than our knees. The mongrel-terrier temperament that belied the adorable brown eyes and silky floppy ears had asserted itself.

He really was the top dog to us kids. A favourite game was to chase and herd us squealing with delight onto someone's bed. His stocky legs never got long enough to jump up himself. Duty done, he would click his toenails proudly down the hardwood hallway from the bedrooms, looking for our mother, to maybe get a treat for his corralling job. He always deferred to Mom, his only leader. As for his bark, when on the job, it could be terrifying, but I never knew him to bite anyone. Not even boyfriends in later years. Those would be enthusiastically harassed and chased away until acceptance was granted, but only after multiple attempts. Once someone became a pack member, however, one could give homage via treats. Cognac was ever the gobble-guts. He enjoyed head and back scratches; cuddling, petting, and nose kisses were also permitted.

Fiendishly smart and capable of many tricks, Cognac was nevertheless loath to perform, except, of course, for treats. He ate anything. In Saskatchewan, where "spits" (sunflower seeds) were consumed by the pound, he could crack and spit out the shells as skillfully as anyone. I once saw him eat leftover stew and pop out the peas, whole. His weakness, though, was garbage. After Labrador, he had to be tied up on our postings, but we still let him out at night to prowl. He prowled for garbage, based on the throwing-up he'd do on his return. Especially if my dad answered the door to let him in. The sight of my dad seemed to make him want to share: "Wow, look what I found and ate tonight!" Often he rolled in it, too. The garbage, not the puke.

Of course Cognac had all his shots, but I don't remember much veterinary care. (Then again, I don't remember much specialized health care for us kids in those days, either.) But there was an instance where he needed some treatment. He'd come limping home unusually subdued, and would only let my mother look. His poor little scrotum had been ripped open. The neighbour's story was that their pet rabbit had delivered a slice with hind-leg claws that caught him in this unfortunate spot. My parents were actually pleased that he had to be neutered, as the hope was it would calm down his territorial habits. Alas, there was no noticeable change in his dominant roaming behaviour at all. The small radar base in Yorkton, Saskatchewan belonged to him. The bartender at the mess said he visited nightly, expecting and receiving his treat. Like a mobster collecting his payola.

More escapes and chases and even arrests by the military police (where we'd have to bail him out from the pound) would follow in the years after Yorkton, on the bigger army base of Petawawa. It was in Petawawa that I myself would marry and leave home, and on return visits, Cognac would always snub me at first, as if to remind me that he hadn't given permission for my departure. He'd come around for his belly rub soon enough, but he did not like to see suitcases.

A final cross-country trip to British Columbia, where my mother would tell me his domain was shrinking with age and arthritis. She still let him out at night, but after a beating by a younger dog down the street, she said he restricted patrols to their own yard, peeing in every corner. She said it was fascinating to finally see his whole nightly routine. And in fact, after one such night, he'd yipped to be let in and sat at my mother's feet for his doggie treat—a healthier tidbit than those of his youthful garbage-eating days. After gobbling it down, he'd looked up at her and tilted his adorable little head, all the golden hairs now bleached with age, then fell over on his round old belly, and lay there, dead. Probably a doggie stroke.

My parents buried Cognac under the rose bushes in their garden at that house in Chilliwack that they'd bought and would sell after my dad left the army. (I wonder if the new owners ever knew? I hope they kept the rose bushes and didn't dig them up!)

As for Cognac, he lives in our family memories. He taught me many lessons that I appreciate even more as I myself age. Live every day to the fullest. Eat garbage while you can. Roam. Explore. Command your world! But learn your limits. There will always be bigger and younger dogs. And in the end, die contentedly after a fun night out and a treat.

One Day in the (Food) Life.

Who likes tables of data? I do, I do! Of course, what we eat changes over our lifetime, over the years, months, even from day to day. Is it a workday? A weekend? A holiday? Are we sick? Are we excited, bored, tired? Are we at home, out-of-town, out with friends? Variety, as they say, is the spice of life, and we all usually eat quite a variety of food in our days.

Here is a daily list of what and when I ate today, tabled as a former organized IT worker can appreciate. Retirement Monday schedule may look a little virtuous, so be sure to keep reading about a different eating day on Casino Wednesday with friends.

Note: Time is given in military hours, a legacy of my upbringing, which is also popular in Québec, where I live now. Plus I used it more often in my computer programming career. I default all my timepieces to this 24-hours format.

Retirement Monday

Daily Notes and Mood	Time	Food	Preparation
Family weekend company left yesterday. Tired of entertaining, restaurants, alcohol. Craving healthy food.	0800–0830	Gourmet Oatmeal	Refer to Breakfast chapter, Gourmet Oatmeal recipe.
Need coffee now.	0900–1000	Coffee	Refer to Coffee chapter.
Prepare lunch.	1000–1030	Spaghetti	Spaghetti sauce: celery, onion, frozen spinach balls, shredded carrot, olives (stuffed with garlic), canned tomatoes, mixed ground beef, pork, garlic powder.
Back from workout at the gym in our building.	1130	Half banana	Cut the banana in half and peel. Force husband to eat the other half.
Lunchtime. Hungry. I missed out on second breakfast today. Not enough time before the gym.	1215–1300	Spaghettini, the skinny spaghetti. I use the "smart" kind with extra fibre. Tastes the same, and I'm always looking for ways to increase fibre intake. Sauce as prepared earlier. Sprinkles of parmesan cheese. Glass of half skim-milk, half almond milk. Leftover almond milk from the weekend guest who likes it. (Janna.)	As prepared earlier by me and cooked up by "guilty-he-didn't-go-to-gym" husband. I like my pasta softer than recommended. This lunch could also have been my supper. We often eat bigger lunches than suppers when at home all day.

Daily Notes and Mood	Time	Food	Preparation
Snack break after errands. At home.	1500–1530	Tea and Lemon loaf slice. Butter the slice. Feels like a real teatime.	Loose leaf expensive oolong Vanilla Orchid. Lemon loaf is from the grocery store bakery. I forgot to serve it for company on the weekend.
Cocktail hour.	1700–1730	Sparkling white wine and orange juice (Mimosa)	Again, leftovers from the weekend guests. Can't let the fizz go to waste.
Supper. Not too hungry. Relaxed. Finally caught up with house chores from the busy weekend.	1730–1800	Chicken noodle soup. Salmon sandwich.	Soup from can. Canned salmon mixed with mayonnaise and chopped up onions. A lighter supper to go with the heavy lunch today.
Evening reading and TV time. The best part of the day.	1900–2200	Wine cocktail.	Refer to Alcohol chapter, Wine Cocktail recipe.

Casino Wednesday

Daily Notes and Mood	Time	Food	Preparation
Usual breakfast. I rarely miss breakfast, no matter what the day's plans.	0800–0830	Whole tangerine. Gourmet Oatmeal.	Refer to Breakfast chapter, Gourmet Oatmeal recipe, except today there's no apples, so I used frozen cherries.
Need coffee now. Again, rare is the day I don't have coffee in the morning.	0900–1000	Coffee	Refer to Coffee chapter.
Lunch. At the Casino with friends.	1200–1300	Soup and Salad bar: veggies, meats, broth, noodles. And salad, mostly pasta salad, tomato based. Red wine.	Self-serve from the buffet.
Coffee break at the Casino.	1500–1530	Coffee	Self-serve at the Casino.
Cocktail hour at home.	1630–1700	Gin and tonic	With lime.
Supper.	1700–1730	Salad and pork chop. Glass of milk.	Leaf lettuce, radishes, celery, mushrooms, green onions, orange peppers. Italian dressing. Pork chops done in oven, baked with prepared barbeque sauce.
Evening reading and TV time and snacks. Home sweet home.	1900–2200	Wine cocktail. Nacho chips and cheese.	Refer to Alcohol chapter, Wine Cocktail recipe. Lactose-free cheese of course.

Notice that I do not list quantities (especially for the wine.) That's because quantities are not important. Eat enough, but not too much. Enjoy, but don't overdo. *Moderation, thy name is my motto!*

Giving Thanks and other Celebrations

Of course, moderation is for the daily grind. We all need to overdo and let loose once in a while, and food is often our favourite way to do so. Christmas, Thanksgiving, Easter. Family reunions. What's the common denominator? Food, of course. A huge spread of overindulgence. In my family's past, a large roasted bird would usually have been served, trimmed around with predictable supplementary dishes. Today, we don't have as many guests living near enough to share such a meal, because my military siblings and elder relatives are spread across the country or around the world. It's rare that I create and serve meals to feed more than my husband and myself, and maybe one son and his family at a time. Yet society and human nature cling to older traditions. I'll do some comparison examples of Then and Now.

First, when my family celebrates has greatly changed over the years. Yes, we still call it Christmas or Thanksgiving, but due to aforementioned distances, the dates we celebrate never quite match what's listed on the calendar for such events anymore.

For example, Christmas 2018 My son Sasha, in the military, was on a deployment overseas and could only get to France in November. What did the rest of us do? Flew from our homes in Alberta and Québec to meet up in Paris for a weekend, is what. A huge restaurant meal together, which had to be at lunchtime at 2:00 p.m. in France, because supper hour there didn't start until 8:00 p.m. Then a jolly walk back in the brisk grey urban air, the gang of us jostling and pairing up, it was back to Sasha and Janna's Airbnb apartment, stopping along the way to buy fine French wine. The boys splurging on a rich, old bottle of scotch. The girls picking out pastries and macarons at the bakery in a rainbow of pale pastel colours and flavours. Then hanging out together for the rest of the day and evening drinking, eating, playing cards. Arguing, laughing, taking pictures. It was a rare time, all of my immediate family together, both sons and their wives. It never felt like a more real Christmas gathering to me, the magic being in the company and the food and drink, not the date.

Another example of disregarding dates to celebrate a holiday: American Thanksgiving, or as we call it, Football Day. Both my sons lived in the United States, gone for the same four years, one for two years of high school and college, the other for the full college experience. As Canadians, my husband and I would always take the Canadian long weekend in early October away from work to visit one or the other son, it not being a holiday weekend yet down south because American Thanksgiving fell in late November. Something about the earlier harvest schedule in Canada, I would assume, accounts for the difference in the country's dates of celebration. Regardless, my boys would not get turkey on Canadian Thanksgiving; in the middle of their school and hockey schedules, we'd be lucky to enjoy one Saturday night meal at a restaurant together. But on American Thanksgiving, which for them was a longer four-day weekend, and which my husband and I didn't get off work, they were stuck down there observing with their American peers. And as pathetic, lonely foreign hockey players, they would always be invited by a school friend's nearby family to partake in American Thanksgiving celebrations. Now, I cannot relate their experiences participating in this iconic American holiday event, but I can tell you it affected my boys considerably. To this day they will take the Thursday and sometimes also the Friday after off from work here in Canada as personal vacation days. D'Arcy hosts a huge football party, my daughter-in-law Jessica decorates the house in American football colours, and everyone wears their NFL jerseys. The table is loaded with snacks and a cooked turkey ready to make bun sandwiches, tailgate-style. Once they even had a "turducken" (turkey stuffed with duck stuffed with chicken), which we had to cross the nearby border into upstate New York to find in a grocery store. I admit I didn't enjoy it; the shredded meat was so over-salted, it burned the tongue.

Many of their friends come to D'Arcy's American Thanksgiving party; some take the day off too, others come after work. My husband and I leave the young people to the never-ending football on TV, and their increasingly rambunctious whooping and cheering as they check their pool picks and scores, and slip away after dessert of homemade cupcakes that someone will have brought.

Of course, food knows no nationality, but times do change. Here's my Canadian Thanksgiving menu comparison from Then, as recalled from what I remember at the large family dinners of my youth, to Now, which is often just a meal with my husband.

Then—cocktail hour: booze, chips and dip, peanuts.

Now—cocktail hour: booze, nachos, shrimp ring, veggies and dip.

Then—large frozen turkey that takes up all the space in the refrigerator for two days, so it can thaw out.

Now—box of chicken breast roast pre-stuffed with bread dressing.

Then—at least five pounds of potatoes to peel. Get the biggest pot out for boiling.

Now—still potatoes, maybe roasted in the pan with the chicken. Or rice, flavoured.

Then—homemade gravy, made on the stovetop in the roasting pan (taking up three burners of room) after the turkey is lifted.

Now—can of sauce, any flavour (like barbeque), ready and heated on the stovetop.

Then—homemade bread dressing, more commonly called stuffing today, with chopped onions and celery and spices from the cupboard. The giblets (the heart, kidney, and liver) from the little bag shoved into the frozen turkey will also be chopped up and put in, as per family recipe.

Now—whatever comes pre-stuffed in the boxed chunk of bird, or, none. Never any giblets anymore. What happened to them?

Then—homemade coleslaw; jellied cranberry sauce; pickled beets.

Now—olives stuffed with garlic.

Then—white buns cooked or warmed in the oven.

Now—baguette fresh from the bakery.

Then—brussels sprouts would have been the exotic vegetable.

Now—Swiss chard and peas mixed with corn and red peppers, or broccoli mixed with carrots, or all of these. More vegetables served today for sure.

Then—pumpkin pie with hand-whipped cream.

Now—pumpkin pie with canned lactose-free whipped cream.

Then—tea with milk and sugar.

Now—coffee with Bailey's Irish cream.

Then—go for a walk; play board games.

Now—watch football on TV. But sometimes, if a son and family are in attendance, we'll still play a game. The daughters-in-law hate when we pull out Trivial Pursuit. We're a pretty competitive family of trivia show-offs.

Then and now—groan with discomfort at too much indulgence and fight for the couch for a nap.

Then and now—two hours later after cleanup, make a turkey or chicken sandwich, and douse with gravy and ketchup. Or eat leftover chips and dip. Or another piece of pie.

Then and now—how much weight does a typical North American gain from Thanksgiving to New Year's? The myths say 5–10 pounds, and although this is not backed up by reliable research, anecdotally, I can imagine it.

Office Food

Food is ever-present, and the office is no exception.

Anyone who's worked in an office environment, especially a government office environment, knows about its kitchen. Basic components are a refrigerator, coffee machine, and a microwave oven. Countertops have plug-ins for optional equipment: toaster, electric kettle, maybe a toaster oven. There is a sink. Cupboards contain paper towels, paper dishes, and plastic cutlery. Dish soap resides under the sink. There also might be a stinky dish towel or two, which I would never touch. Some office kitchens I encountered (as a consultant, I encountered a variety of them in the recesses of those large concrete blocks of government buildings), were also called lunchrooms, because they were large enough for a couple of tables and chairs, but these were rare. Mostly, the kitchens were just kitchens, not a place to consume anything prepared there. We ate at our desks or sometimes in a boardroom during "working lunches," where complaints about crumbs and cleanup would be made from those who attended the 1:00 p.m. meetings. Personally, I either ate my lunch at my desk after a midday walk or swim or gym workout, or I went out to commercial locales for lunches of Vietnamese soup or Chinese food, favourites that I won't make myself. This is not to say I didn't visit the office kitchen for daily coffee, tea, or snack breaks, where people would leave cookies or have fund-raising chocolate for sale. Of course I did, to hang out and escape the cubicle once in a while, as did we all. Random meetups to chat, to read notice boards; gossip and venting; much power-tripping was expressed in that little room.

A major source of drama in the kitchen was cleanup duty. Multitudes of notes:

"Don't leave dirty dishes in the sink!"
"Wipe the counters!"
"The microwave stinks—wash it after use!"
"We all share this space, don't be such pigs!!!" Many exclamation marks, many exhortations and threats.

"A note to whoever used my coffee cream, I hope you enjoyed the big gob of spit I did in it."

Yes, I really read this last note taped to the refrigerator door one afternoon when I went to get my pasta salad from the fridge. I don't know if someone really did spit in their own creamer container to discourage borrowers from helping themselves, but seriously, it was a reminder that coworkers might not be your best friends, nor even any kind of friendly folk. I was so shaken by this note (no saint myself, I've "borrowed" from the office fridge, I'll admit), I went immediately downstairs to the shops and purchased a two-dollar pint of coffee cream. My own note read, *Help yourself. Please buy the next one.* There's a lesson here somewhere.

I actually witnessed an almost physical fight in the kitchen once. The refrigerator was due for cleaning. The smell was becoming an office priority. Every time the fridge door was opened, the odour of sour milk and rotting meat sandwiches, furred with grey-green molds, would waft down the corridors, permeating the floor. The volunteer cleanup crew had posted a note to remove all items by 4:00 p.m. the night before. Of course, not everyone did. So, Teresa, always self-appointed volunteer-in-chief, had removed all of the food remains to the counters the next morning. Then an offender walked in.

"What the hell do you think you're doing, what's going on, who moved my lunch to the counter?" Scott demanded. Scott was usually a quiet guy; he sat in a corner cubicle and would complain about bosses and politics anytime you stopped by to say hello, but normally he kept to himself. He was over six feet tall and filled the doorway. I was stuck on the far side of the room at the coffee counter. Terry straightened from the open door of the fridge, rag in hand.

"Hey, we're cleaning the fridge. Don't be a jerk. Why was your lunch left over from yesterday anyway? We put up a note."

"None of your friggin' business. I can't believe

you touched my lunch!" And he picked it up from the counter and moved to push past Teresa, trying to put it back on the fridge shelf.

"Scott, what are you doing, the power's off, don't put it back. We're cleaning it, can't you read?" Her voice rose to an uncomfortable squeal, and a few people were peering around Scott now from outside the doorway.

"It'll go bad...get out of the way, it has to be refrigerated!" His own voice was rising.

We didn't see what was in the plastic Tupperware-type container in Scott's hand, but his reaction seemed extreme.

He continued, "I swear, Terry, get the hell out of my way!"

He started towards her, she was backing away from the fridge, the hand holding the rag raised in a protective reflex.

I myself now stepped forward, using my old commanding lifeguard voice (which shows up at such interesting times), "Scott, relax!"

In the same moment, another guy stepped in from the hall and put his hand on Scott's shoulder. (Thank goodness...Jason was another tall coworker. What did I think I was going to do?) Scott froze in place. He looked confused, then clutching his container to his chest, without another word, he turned and pushed past Jason into the hallway and scuttled off to his cubicle. Teresa started to shake and sputter and mumble. People moved off. I stayed and helped her, shaky rag in hand, to finish cleaning the fridge. All to say, coworkers can be a strange lot. Don't mess with their food.

Christmas at the Office

Christmas and holidays in general necessarily involve food. Celebration, life: food is the common denominator across all cultures. I've mentioned my own traditional English upbringing, but I don't identify today as sticking to this one food culture. The turkey with traditional trimmings of gravy and cranberry sauce of my childhood has evolved to include any kind of expensive chunks of meat with varieties of different trimmings. Lamb with rosemary roasted potatoes. Huge vats of chili. Sausages in mini buns. All with vegetables of any colour, vegetables that I'd never heard of in my youth, like kohlrabi and bok choi. Dips, spicy and exotic. Shredded coleslaw salads in rainbow cabbage hues. We certainly never had purple carrots or orange cauliflower growing up, but food today, like most of life, has expanded to be multi-coloured and more vibrant, more interesting.

Food, life, and holidays, cannot be divorced from the extra-intense emotions of the times they force us to associate. Expectations can be high; relationships spark and sizzle or fizzle. Families sometimes only get together at such times, dredging up past hurts or wrongs as if they had happened only yesterday, not yesteryears ago. The following story is about how such emotional times can be intensified, by an innocent pizza, no less.

"Welcome back, Teresa, you've been away awhile. Hope all is well?"

Teresa over-laughed her response of, "Oh yes, I'm fine, all is great, life is great, I feel fine. Really, nothing to talk about, hahaha!"

Shuffling off in the background, other coworkers slunk away to their cubicles, leaving me alone with Teresa—"Don't call me Terry"—in the doorway to my own little corner niche. Unable to escape, I pursued.

"So, what have they got you doing now? You were trying to get the Business Analyst position, last year was it? Did they fill it? Do you still want it?"

Teresa had been a quality assurance analyst until her sudden leave just after Christmas ten months ago, a permanent employee at this federal government department in downtown Ottawa, where I was consulting as a Database Administrator. We didn't work directly together, but she represented at many of the same project meetings, and as two of the few women in this male-dominated Information Technology division, we often sat together and chatted at the meetings. She was a perfectionist, often staying late at work, and would stubbornly refuse to give her QA stamp of approval on software until she felt it was ready, which often meant never, or at least until she was ordered to give it. This endeared her to the developers, who slacked off on their own testing, knowing that Teresa would dig up all the problems for them, but it frustrated her bosses, the Project Managers, who resented the extensions of deadlines because of her thoroughness, which they called "obsessive-excessive." I personally agreed that she took her role seriously to a fault, but she was not my area of concern, and she was nice enough, if a little different from me in her personal style. Her cubicle had pictures of puppies, she wore dresses, and her hair was always professionally coloured. We had little in common outside of work. I wore jeans with plain blouses, and styling my hair consisted of washing it once a day or twice if I swam at lunchtime, so it was always short. I worked with many men and my style blended in well, like camouflage.

"You know, Michele, I'm on anxiety medication now. I'm doing better, my son started high school this fall, and I'm only working four days a week to ease back in. They gave me the BA position, though, so I start that after training with Jan for a while."

"That's nice. I have to check my database logs now. See you at the status meeting this afternoon, okay?"

And she popped away; I couldn't tell if she was offended at my cutting the chat short or not.

My coworker-boss, Aaron, came by later.

"I see Terry's back in the office. How is she? Still crazy?"

"Come on, don't call her Terry; she hates that. And she's not 'crazy,' Aaron, but she says she feels better. She looks good, I think she needed the rest. She got remarried last year just before Christmas, remember? Then her son got rebellious. She's had a tough time."

"Yeah, I know. Christmas? She left right after that, didn't she? I hope that pizza thing didn't send her over the edge. Remember?"

"No, what pizza thing?"

"You know, the email about the office Christmas potluck. Terry was organizing it. We decided to have some fun and messed with her a bit."

"What are you talking about? I took a couple weeks off before Christmas last year, so didn't go to the office party. What happened?"

It turns out, Teresa had had a meltdown at the office Christmas party. She had listed items in an email and people were supposed to let her know which of them they would bring. Things like shortbread cookies, tortières, eggnog, other traditional or special dishes. Many of the office staff, especially the women, replied. But the guys in the office got together and decided they'd rather order pizza from their favourite lunchtime deli and have it delivered. And they did, to Teresa's horror. I understand that she stomped out of the boardroom, all decorated with red and green tinselly garlands for the event, and didn't return to work after holidays in January. She was off. For ten months.

"So, it was you guys who freaked her out, and she was on stress leave for ten months?" I was flabbergasted.

"I guess so. Whatever. Hey, I can't make the meeting this afternoon, be sure to take notes for me."

How considerate, in every way; it wasn't my turn to take notes. Lesson. Again. The office is not your friend. Don't bring your own issues about Christmas or food. The office will eat you alive.

On a positive note, Terry did get her new position, which came with a promotion. Sometimes I believe in karma.

Desserts

I haven't discussed a major food group much yet: dessert. We know it as sweets, cookies, baked goods, really any kind of starchy sugary concoction that is served after supper or sometimes even after lunch. Dessert wasn't and isn't an important meal component for me; I prefer eating dessert-type foods in their own stand-alone timeslot, and not appended to an existing meal. I grew up with the idea that dessert was something special, not a regular thing. For birthdays, for example, with the birthday-ee getting to pick what kind of cake Mom would make. Chocolate, especially Black Forest Cake, was popular, but I requested angel food cake, with whipped cream (Ah, those pre-dairy-problem days of youth!) and strawberries. Canned frozen strawberries made watery extra sauce which the spongy angel food would absorb into a nice pink cake bite. Use the cake as bread to mop it up. Dip a large swipe of whipped cream. Heavenly. (So, that's how it got its name.) My favourite.

Most of our birthday cakes included money baked into the pieces: nickels, dimes, the occasional quarter. My husband's family also did this. I did it earlier for my own children, but it seems to be a tradition that runs in streaks for some people, for some amount of time. I do plan to re-initiate it for my grandchildren, but will probably have to use loonies and toonies (Canadian one- and two-dollar coins) for them, as a quarter becomes the new nickel in our inflated generation. It is an interesting tradition, and trying to research the beginnings are slippery; many cultures mention some variation of it.

My preferred origin story is this one: In Greece, baking money into cakes or bread was done to celebrate St. Basil's day, on January 1. St. Basil was an early influence in the Christian church, known for his work with the poor and underprivileged. My own theory, therefore, is that the money was put into bread and handed out to the poor who would certainly appreciate both the bread and the monetary handout. It's a nice theory; how it got to birthday cakes for middle class kids is why I enjoy questioning food traditions. There's always an interesting story behind them. In fact, some people also bake a non-monetary item into their cakes, like a button. Depending on the story you choose to believe and pass along, finding the button in your piece means either you are the fool, the sucker who didn't get any money, or that it was the luckiest piece to get, being the one and only. My mother must have not wanted to risk one of her four kids not getting any money, hence, we never had the button in any of our birthday cakes. And whoever got only a nickel would always beg for another piece of cake, of course.

So, cake, or pie—my father insisted on apple pie for his birthday dessert, with a slice of cheddar cheese on top—was really the only kind of mealtime desserts I grew up with. Ice cream, cookies, candy, puddings, sugared fruit cups: these were snack foods, eaten after school or before bedtime or snuck anytime between regularly scheduled meals. It is the pattern I follow today, usually at afternoon teatime, either at home or out, with friends or alone, reading or writing. And never anything I myself have baked because a world of options awaits at the local coffee shop: pecan bars, Nanaimo squares, ginger cookies, chocolate chip muffins, and rice crispie squares. Someone asked me why I would pay five dollars for a rice crispie square, when I could make a couple dozen at home for that price. Well, you've read my diet chapter. I figure one square is all my figure should afford.

𝒟rink, 𝒟rink

Drinks are, of course, an every-present part of some people's consumption, mine included. By drinks, I don't mean glasses of water or milk or pop served with meals. (Yes, pop, not soda, is what I call carbonated drinks like Coke.) I mean drinks for drinking's sake. As a food. As its own reward, so to speak.

Pop was never a standalone beverage in our home. It was mostly used as a mix for my parents' alcohol, and it was Coke, 7-Up, or Ginger Ale only. Or the same pop choices were a treat at the movie theatre with popcorn. It could be bought with allowance money outside the home, but I didn't choose it often over chocolate or crayons. The first place I remember drinking pop for true pleasure was as a little kid, maybe six, in Calgary, getting root beer at A&W. What a flavour! I can't describe it now other than as tasting like root beer, but then, poured over ice cream as a float, it was scrumptious, a vanilla smoothness and fizzy eruption releasing delicate aromas that I can still taste in memory. My mouth waters just describing it. But when I was seven, my sergeant father got moved with his family to Germany. No root beer there in the mid-1960s, if I recall correctly. What they had in Germany was Fanta. Orange and Grape. The orange was so juicy and orange-y that it conjured Christmas with each sip. But it felt so "spicy" how the carbonation hurt my mouth, I never really became an addict. In fact, if I could get away with it, I'd shake the glass bottle to get rid of the fizz, but of course, this was tricky if you didn't want to lose most of it through the resulting explosion. It was not a manoeuvre one could handle in the movie theatre, for example, which was where I drank my pop. By the time I lived in Goose Bay, I still didn't like pop much. Once in a while, I'd buy a Tahiti Treat can from the pop machine at the base movie theatre to sip throughout the movie. It was pink cream soda. I can still remember the can design, white with pink and green palm trees.

Then, I discovered the pop-dispensing machine at the American-side movie theatre. (The United States had a big Air Force base in Goose Bay in the late 1960s.) Their concession offered ten times the selection of our Canadian-side theatre concession. Chocolate bars and candy lined a wall, colourful and foreign, especially having just come from post-war Germany. I had my first Butterfinger chocolate bar there. The Americans had a soda-pop tank, not unlike those of today, that you pushed little metal levers to release the choice of liquid into your own paper cup. It seemed a wonderful idea to pour your own, and I soon invented (well, everyone did) "swamp water" at the soda-pop machine. A little splash of coke. Add some orange. Ginger ale. Even some water to cut the carbonation, for me. No ice, again, for me. Wonderful! And different every time.

I wouldn't drink much more pop in my youth until diet drinks hit the shelves and young women of my time were expected to be thin, ridiculous as that was. Tab and Fresca arrived. Again, too fizzy for me, and the Fresca could melt your teeth with acidity. But at least, along with skim milk, drinks were becoming available as lighter on calories. I admit that I sometimes drank these pops for taste. I did like the tinny tang in the diet drinks of that time, before they stopped using saccharin due to bladder cancer studies in rats. As if aspartame was any better for you.

As a young mother in the 1980s, fruit drinks and juices were still popular to feed our children, not like today when juice is considered a sugary "evil." By fluke, I was ahead of the curve then to cut the apple juice with water, admittedly because I myself found it too sweet, not because I was some kind of anti-sugar advocate. I've already mentioned my first son also disliked too much sweet, so he wouldn't drink juice at full strength, anyway. So it was with D'Arcy that I developed versions of a new kind of swamp water.

"Mommy, Daddy's gone to school. Can we have our 'special drink' now, please?"

It was a Tuesday evening, and Don was finishing up his university degree with night classes after work, after supper, after baby Sasha was asleep for the first half of his night, before midnight feeding. It was Mommy and D'Arcy's special hour in Winnipeg, Manitoba in 1990.

"Okay, get the juice and pop from the fridge; I'll get the glasses." Big tall plastic patio-style ones with colourful patterns. Probably full of BPA: bisphenol—a chemical additive to food containers that eventually would be banned from plastic baby bottles due to hormonal influences. Blissfully unaware of that and bladder cancer risks, I reached above D'Arcy to the freezer for the tray of ice cubes. He was pulling the pop out from the fridge. At almost four years old he was big and strong and could easily handle the 2-litre bottle of Diet Coke even when it was full.

"More ice, Mommy! I want four."

I set the ice tray down and reached above the sink to the cabinet containing the Bacardi. I didn't mind a lot of ice in my rum and coke myself.

"Get the lime and lemon from the fridge, now, honey. No, don't get the knife! I'll do that!" I poured the coke and rum (no rum in D'Arcy's, I wasn't that bad of a mother) in our glasses over the ice. I put the ice tray back in the top freezer shelf, noting that the freezer needed defrosting again. (Yes, I was that bad of a housekeeper that it was a task that always needed doing.)

Lemon and lime slices squeezed and added, orange or grapefruit juice or both added to D'Arcy's "special drink," everything put back in the fridge, off we headed to the basement family room to settle down in front of the TV on the futon we used as a guest bed, propped up with blankets to snuggle and TV tables on the sides, where we set our drinks. Our favourite weekly ritual show, *Tour of Duty*, was about to start. D'Arcy and Mommy settled in for our hour, sipping and singing along to the theme song, "Paint it Black" before all the cool army and action scenes of the episode.

Years pass. "Paint it Black" got redone as a Rolling Stones cover by Gob. D'Arcy moved out and into his own home to start his own family. Don and I now get together nightly for a few hours of TV before bed, in our condo, on our nice leather couches and comfy chairs. I don't need the blankets to snuggle anymore, like I did in the basement in Winnipeg, but I still like to. And before we settle, I mix us each a special drink, mine a wine cocktail nowadays, and (expensive) pure cherry juice and diet lemonade for him. Ice from the frost-free fridge—thank goodness for progress in appliances. With added lemon slices and frozen cherries. A coworker once mentioned that cherries were good for people prone to gout. I've always known that what we eat can be medicinal, but sometimes Don still suffers from gout anyway.

And although I've mentioned them in this story, alcoholic drinks, like coffee, deserve their own section.

Alcohol

Like most people, I've had my own love-hate relationship with alcohol. As a child, I watched the adults around me drink alcohol. (I use the term "adults" loosely—my parents were teenagers when I was born.) As with cigarettes and coffee, alcohol was off-limits to children. That didn't stop us from observing and learning. I deduced that smoking and drinking were stupid, especially the smoking, which went on nonstop, all day, anywhere. Stinky, dirty, I hated the smoking. Unlike my brothers, and most of my peers at any age, I never smoked.

Drinking seemed a little different. It was never

done during the day, or during the workweek. It was saved for weekends, in the evenings, after supper and chores and duties. It was anticipated as a fun thing to do and usually was done with a recreational activity. My parents never drank alone; they always included others and when we visited friends or extended family, the adults drank there, too. My father drank when he took us trick or treating at Hallowe'en ("trick or beer"), and neighbours invited adults over for drinks when they barbequed. People seemed happy when they drank, and the drinking always went with fun food like pretzels and popcorn, or if at mealtime, those meals would be special, like barbequed hot dogs, corn on the cob, and salads made from Jello. Celebratory meals were their own category and included their own special alcohol. My parents would drink sparkly wine with orange juice in the morning for Christmas.

As a child, then, I remember alcohol as something to look forward to when I grew up. It was natural as teenagers that most of my friends (yes, and I) tried drinking alcohol, usually beer. It was in those years that I learned: 1) the negative effects of drinking and, 2) the very negative effects of drinking. Beer never tasted good to me, and I was always stomach-sick from it the next day, even after only one or two.

So followed the throwing up, the stinking beer breath, the hangovers, the rowdy friends. I never became a big drinker in my youth. Nor even in college. Married by then, my husband Don and I were still too strapped to afford much better than shared pitchers of beer on weekends at the pubs. By then, I'd discovered cocktails were much better tasting, but pricier. I would order them only at a fancy dinner out, say for an anniversary. I vowed that once I got a good job after college, I'd never drink beer again, only cocktails. And I never did. Rum and diet coke became my drink of choice. A little lime in it, please, à la Cuba libre.

It's true that the richer I became, the more I drank. It tasted good, it felt good, and I had enough self-control to drink just to the point where I wouldn't be sick from it. Alas, like my own parents discovered later in life, I too would discover the insidious problems with alcohol.

My doctor—not the same young lady doctor of my youth, but apparently with the same medical-school sensitivity training—said to his assistant when I admitted my weekly quantities of alcohol on the checkup form: "Oh, let's see here—wow. Look at this; this one's a drinker." And then he said to me, "So, why do you drink so much? Are you anxious? Do you self-medicate?"

Huh? Self-medicate? I was working as an IT consultant with a stressful job and had two teenaged boys in competitive hockey. My husband was having his own medical issues with back problems. We were at the peak of life's middle-aged problems. What was self-medication? It sounded like a good thing to me, to be honest.

But the truth was, it wasn't a good thing. I needed to cut back. I was developing too much of a taste and realized it. I'm not a saint, though, so instead of quitting completely, I became "my own liquor control board" (I never forgot this old Ontario liquor board slogan), and I switched to wine. With wine, I could cut back the alcohol content while still enjoying what I considered to be the benefits.

And life did settle down. The children grew up, moved on to their own lives and their own relationships with alcohol (such is the circle of life) and my reasons for self-medication settled down. Today, I enjoy a glass of wine when at a restaurant with friends. I admit I still like to drink in the evenings, even by myself. (I think George Thorogood even had a song about that.) I can further cut the alcohol content by making wine cocktails. Not so good with the calories, but we all make trade-offs.

Wine cocktail recipe

I hope this is a drink to enjoy well into later life!

As with coffee, I have favourite drinking vessels for my wine, usually souvenir glasses from trips to wineries. I like to reminisce about where I got them when I drink from them. Not too small, but not too big; you may want a refill.

- Red wine. Your choice. I like the vanilla-tasting California reds myself. I will sample it before mixing in the rest of the ingredients, as the taste of the wine will influence my proportions. For example, vanilla-y wines don't like as much lemon added, but the fruity,

lighter Italian or French wines do. That's all I got, I'm no sommelier.
- Cranberry-cherry juice
- 100% cherry juice
- Sparkling lemonade (diet, gotta cut back somewhere!)
- Slice of lemon
- 3-4 frozen cherries
- Ice cube

This drink can be too sweet. If so, adjust for more wine. Or use some of those new sparkling flavoured waters. Of course, as always, "Cheers!"

Generations and Change

On a recent out-of-town visit to my son and daughter-in-law, we were tired from our trip and didn't want to go to a restaurant for supper upon our arrival. But both Sasha and Janna work full-time. I felt guilty about asking what was scheduled for our supper and was even ready to throw on a quick soup and bread meal for the four of us.

"No worries, Mom, we'll just order in."

Hmm. I didn't order pizza or Chinese food much anymore because of the lactose intolerance and salt-aversion thing, so I hesitated. They didn't notice.

"So, what do you feel like having? Thai? Vegetarian? Greek? Barbeque? Hamburgers? Italian?" Janna recited a long list of food types and world geography that left me dizzy.

Don and I looked at each other and just shrugged. "What do you mean? Where do you order from that has all that kind of food?"

"Oh, all the restaurants around here in Edmonton have food delivery, you know, like SkiptheDishes, UberEats, whatever. So, pick a place and make an order. They'll deliver."

Confused, dazed, like an alien on a new planet, I mumbled, "I don't know, whatever you would normally order for yourselves if we weren't here? What do you want?"

"Okay, we'll get dinner from that Indian place we like, right, Sasha? I'll just double our usual order."

And then we had a drink. Like we can now, the young adults could already afford to keep a stocked bar on hand at home. We chatted to catch up with lives that are lived provinces—and lifestyles and generations—apart. The food arrived, hot and wafting warm spices I didn't recognize. Don volunteered to pay, but no, it had been already taken care of when we ordered using the "app." Thanks, anyway, Dad. Then it was dished out onto plates and cutlery from the kids' apartment. Hardly any cleanup after, either. I was impressed. Of course, I didn't see the bill and am glad of it. I'm sure I would've sounded even more like my own mother when she discovered that I didn't peel potatoes for every supper: *Must be nice to be so rich that you can have instant rice or pasta so often instead of cheaper potatoes,* was what she really thought.

That's funny, I also remember Grandma sniffing in disapproval about how thick my mother peeled her potatoes, mentioning that it must be nice to be so rich that you can waste so much! The situations of generational judgement change with time, but not the attitude, so it seems. As I myself had recently learned having supper ordered in at my son's. *It must be nice,* I thought!

Despite the end-of-world naysayers—you know them, "overpopulation, not enough food, don't have more children"—my personal observation of my and my childrens' situations is that there is access to more food and more food variety than in my family's previous generations. I vaguely remember times when food was not securely guaranteed, though only from my parents' admonishments. As children, we were made to clean our plates, not allowed to leave the family dinner table until everything was eaten. We were threatened with visions of starving children in far-away lands, but looking back, I realize that those visions probably came from not-so-distant personal family history, from old-world immigrant grandparents, when their own food was not always so secure and starvation was a spectre for most of the world.

Times would change, but food cultures sometimes hang on past their best-before date. The trick is knowing when they've served their usefulness and can be ditched. As in this story:

"Excuse me," my brother Mark giggled after letting loose a huge burp at the chrome dinette table in our eat-in kitchen of our Calgary PMQ.

I burst out laughing; at six years old, a loud, rumbling burp is the funniest joke. At the sudden noise and polite expletive, my mother came running back into the kitchen. The comment hadn't been meant to ask to be excused from the table, as Mom obviously had thought. Mark and I hadn't, wouldn't, or couldn't finish whatever supper concoction Mom had been forcing us to eat, and had given up to go feed our baby brother in the living room. Dad? There were many dinners without Dad, who was probably away on army training somewhere. My young mother was so hopeful now, looking us over, looking at our plates.

"Who finished their supper? Who asked to be excused?"

Mark and I looked at each other and burst out laughing again.

"Oh, you kids! You're not leaving that table until you both finish!" We couldn't help it, we were rolling on the slippery vinyl chairs now, all drama and happily shrieking uncontrollably. Poor mom, she was trying so hard.

"I don't care if you have to sit there all night!" But now, her face quivered, too, and then it happened. Mom started laughing with us.

An historical food tradition had just bitten the dust. Yes, times change, thank goodness. I don't remember being forced to clean up a plate after that.

I also remember my parents as being the last generation who remembered that food necessary for life had been grown at home in private gardens. My grandmother had a double-lot-sized garden at her house in town when she was in her nineties. She watered, weeded, then plundered and harvested all the edibles to bottle, pickle, jelly and jam them, using preservation methods from a childhood that depended on such products to survive prairie winters. Rows of jars lined hand-made plank shelving in the basement: pickled cucumbers, beets, beans, pickled everything, really. There were sweets like apricot and apple compotes in addition to all the jams. These mason jars were like sums in a bank account in my grandmother's time, promising food and plenty for months to come. My own parents, raising children in a different world and lifestyle of military moving, nevertheless still baked bread and certainly dessert items like cakes and cookies and pies from scratch. These were the years of sending kids to the neighbours to borrow an egg or a cup of sugar. And even they put in a small plot of vegetables in the community garden when we lived in locales hospitable to do so, like in Saskatchewan. But by then, the wild rhubarb for pies and the one good feed of corn and couple of potatoes that this little garden produced for a family of six, had become just a fun family activity, and the weeding we kids were forced to do never carried the same life and death importance that my own parents' generation experienced. As teens, we wouldn't even help out anymore, not being able to see any point to it. We didn't need this home-grown food to survive; it was a leftover routine from a disappearing frontier culture. Even I myself as a young mother in Winnipeg (where every backyard has rich black soil that can still produce more zucchini and tomatoes than one family can eat without sharing or preserving) had a little garden for the boys to help out in after work and daycare. But again, it was just an echo of a times gone by.

The last food garden I ever planted was in Aylmer, Québec, where the boys planted pumpkin seeds to be ready for Hallowe'en. Alas, a younger cousin had visited in September and plucked them too early, small and green off the vine. Amid the tears—this was a good lesson on life and death for little boys—I promised to buy them the biggest, best pumpkins from Loblaws to replace them. In hindsight, I guess replacement was not a good lesson on lost life, but what can you do? The best you can, is all.

Interestingly, my daughter-in-law Jessica, now grows herbs in her own growing family's backyard. I had a gin and tonic there recently; the ice cubes had little mint leaves frozen inside. Mint leaves from her own backyard. The next generation might not need food they grow themselves to survive, but they are learning that local can be better for taste, for self-satisfaction, even for bigger global reasons. Just because I'm aging into the new vintage generation doesn't mean I can't adapt; I'm happy to be learning and moving along with the times. It's fun to notice how what's old is new again. And today when my young grandson burps and laughs, I can still see the humour in it. Some things don't change.

Retirement

Speaking of getting older, here's an anecdote about how living together, and eating together, full-time in retirement can work out. Or sometimes not.

"Oh my god. I eat like a woman!"

So growled my husband Don, pushing the shopping cart down the aisle in the big grocery store one late afternoon. It was a typical retirement summer day for us: with an appointment in Ottawa to meet a financial advisor earlier in the day, followed by some shopping at a nearby mall (shopping for me, Don waiting in the food court with a coffee and muffin and his e-reader). Then lunch at our favourite Vietnamese noodle soup place, before heading back across the river to beat the rush hour traffic on the bridges. We'd also stop at the local Provigo (Québec's version of Loblaws, our biggest chain grocery store in the area) to pick something up for supper; we always carried our reusable bags in the car for these errands. In fact, we rarely shopped in bulk anymore because living in downtown Aylmer with three or four grocery stores within walking distance, as well as multiple drugstores and two French bakeries, meant meals could be assembled daily from short walks to pick up ingredients. Very old world.

As usual, I didn't think twice about making all the decisions about the evening's supper menu. I figured that since we'd just eaten lunch out at a restaurant, we didn't need a heavy meal that night.

"I think it's time for chicken. Let's do the chicken and salad tonight. I have all the salad things at home, even the leaf lettuce to mix with the Boston lettuce. Chicken breasts, right?" I wandered to the chicken section along the lengthy meat aisle corridor and poked around. But the breasts were packaged too large for the two of us, I figured, and I prefer the darker cuts, relatively speaking. Even dark chicken meat seems lighter today than when I was younger.

"Here's skinless, boneless chicken thighs, Don," I said, just as Don was picking up a package of turkey breast meat.

"Hey, let's do turkey instead," he said.

"No!" I barked. Having already imagined the meal in my head, I didn't want to consider any changes.

Since we were there anyway, we liked to browse the rest of the aisles for store specials because we didn't get to Provigo as often as the walking-distance stores. Only this time, Don was sulky and not participating in our outing with his usual zeal. (I exaggerate with the *zeal*, but he still was being sulky.)

"What's wrong?" I asked.

And that's when he mumbled, "I eat like a woman. Skinless, boneless chicken...salad, whatever!"

What? My first reaction was anger, as in what

the hell does that mean, to eat like a woman? Sure sounds derogatory to me.

"Okay, then if you don't like what I make for supper, make whatever you want for yourself!"

"Yeah, well, no thanks. That's why I put up with it because I don't know what to make. I only wanted to try the turkey instead of chicken today, that's all, but no, you have to have it all your own way! I never get to pick out anything."

Despite the silliness of how it sounds now, like a mommy fighting with her child, this complaint was fair, and once I calmed down, I knew it.

Retirement, like any stage of life, has its challenges as circumstances evolve. Life changes; we need to change with it. I've always been a planner, and try to control what I can, but I needed to loosen up about my new retirement role as chief chef in the household.

We kept the chicken thighs, though; neither of us wanted to walk back to the meat section. This store was acres large. I apologized as best I could. And now I try to be more careful to let Don plan more of the home meals, or at least let him think he's planning them. But not too often.

He really isn't as good at it as I am.

Grandma

Food. Life. As we begin, so we end.
This story is not 100% true. I wasn't in the room during this story, but it is my own version of how it transpired, as told to me by others who were.

The room was small but cozy, home-made afghan blankets, some knitted, others crocheted, done by Grandma herself or more likely, gifted by daughters-in-law to warm up the rest-home atmosphere. Some in sedate blues or greens, some in cheerful reds and oranges, all faded with the strong prairie sunshine that flooded through the picture window in all seasons. Not today; shades were drawn to keep lighting low, to allow Grandma some quiet in her last hours.

Just one grandchild of dozens, I sat my turn in the guest chair near the door, as scores of others—nieces, nephews, in-laws, friends—came and went in hushed respect over these past few days. The old velour couch was reserved for the sons and daughters, my uncles and aunts, one of whom was always by her bedside, patting her arm, holding her hand. Such a tiny old woman. She'd always been an old woman to me, but now, when she was well past 90, I realized how much younger she must have once been, on my many childhood visits. Vibrant even. Taking me with her to get her hair coloured, "Chocolate Kiss" the name of the tint. She always commented that I was so lucky, such warm brown eyes and rich brown hair. Her natural colouring was, as she put it, "Thin mousy hair and watery blue eyes." Not true, Grandma, your eyes always twinkled for me. Although maybe not today, not anymore.

I remember Grandma's cooking. Of course I remember her pies, raspberry jelly (not the jam, she strained those annoying seeds out in cheesecloth), big farmer lunches of roasts, hams, always potatoes and gravy, and always at least three or four desserts. There'd been roly-poly, a pastry made with suet and brown sugar. I would someday recognize it again as *pets de soeur* in my adopted home of Québec. Muffins. Her famous apple pie, as flaky as my own mother made, which is saying something. I remember Grandma showing teenage-me how to make pie crust. I mentioned that my mother made it so well that no point in learning how, it wouldn't be as good as my mother's. Yes, smart-mouthed me. Shocked, she said, "Someday you'll be the old mother and will have to make pie for your family!" I never did take enough interest to learn it well. And truthfully I've never had pie as good as my mother's nor my grandmother's. But she was right about one thing, I did become the old mother. Just with different things to pass along. Because I learned more from Grandma than how to make pie crust.

I learned how to hold your family together, that love is not the only ingredient. Patience, consistent communication—in times before our interconnected world, this meant hand-written letter-writing—and constant attention are needed. There were years of busy family-of-my-own life, but Grandma always wrote, starting with, "I haven't heard from you in a while, please write back." What might have begun as guilt, prompted replies; usually phone calls were quicker for my generation (like texts are now for my own children to keep in touch). But keep in touch we did, until, by the end, she was more than missed, she was kept in my heart always. As my own mother is kept and missed, and as I expect and hope my own children and grandchildren will learn, and keep, and pass along lessons of life to the next generations, to evolve, to change, to make better.

Like her meals, and baking, and cooking, Grandma taught me life is more than the ingredients. It's how, with our personal touches, we put it all together.

That last day of her life, Grandma asked for, and ate, spoonfuls of butterscotch pudding, a favourite treat.

First, and last, we eat.

Author's Afterword and Acknowledgements

Book two! I'd always wanted to write a book, and after the success of my first memoir, *Camp Follower One Army Brat's Story*, my lifetime dream seemed fulfilled. After that publication, retirement moved along to include other hobbies: reading, joining a curling league, becoming a new grandmother, blogging, travelling with Don, visiting family. And more reading. Life was busy and good.

Then something started nagging at me. I'd written a book, yes. Check. But was that all there was? What about all the other stories and ideas bubbling throughout my day and life? Readers of *Camp Follower* started asking, "When's the next one?" This had come as a shock. It had taken over a year to write a book people could read in hours, and then they wanted more right away? What had I gotten into? Was the first book just that, an only book? What about the fiction? I read fiction, wasn't I going to write any?

I'm happy to say, this second book has resolved

many doubts for me. I can and did write this next book, another memoir kind like the first, true enough. But I've also been writing some fiction short stories, one of a *Twilight Zone* style that was published in the Ottawa Writers Group 2019 anthology under my social media name of Stevie Szabad. I've started other works, even a novel, and we'll see where they lead me.

As always, I thank my husband Don for his partnership and support for all things I undertake, including my writing. It's not easy living with a writer, who can and will use anything about anyone in a story.

I thank my writers groups and fellow authors who I've met both in person and online. It's been a new world for me to belong to such an inspiring community.

Note about the Cognac story: A version of this story was first published in the anthology *My Hero Dog, Stories of How our Dogs Have Helped Shape who We Are,* edited by Circe Olson Woessner for the Museum of the American Military Family.

Editing, cover art, layout, printing: Cait Gordon, Nathan Fréchette, Eric Desmerais. I'm grateful to have found such professional help to produce a quality product for the most important people to this author—the readers.

Special appreciation: I've been touched by the feedback, emails, and messages from the readers of *Camp Follower.* Your support and encouragement convinced me that I had more stories to tell, and this book is dedicated (after Don) to you.

Thanks for reading.

About the Author

Michele is retired from careers as a Database Administrator, computer programmer, and lifeguard. She was born in Calgary, Alberta, but grew up on military bases in both Canada and Germany, and now lives with her retired Air Force husband of over 40 years, Don, in Aylmer, Québec. Besides her writing, she loves hiking, sports, music, and travelling. And family. A reader since her mother first tossed magazines in her crib, she still loves all kinds of books, and will continue writing as either herself, Michele Sabad, or as her social media persona of Stevie Szabad. Follow Michele's writing on her author website stevieszabad.com.

www.ingramcontent.com/pod-product-compliance
Lightning Source LLC
LaVergne TN
LVHW051519070426
835507LV00023B/3198